The FLOWER
Mainly called the "BUD", the flower is the fruit of the female cannabis plant and is made up of calyxes to form a dense nuggety bud head called a Cola. Containing the most cannabinoids it is sought after for medical advantages and recreational fun. The male produces flowers with pollen.

The SUGAR LEAVES
These leaves are small, full of trichomes, and are located close to calyx bud's.

The INTER-NODES
Are the node points where leaves, branches, and the calyx bud's form.

The FAN LEAVES
The big leaves - all leaves are important to the plants development but the fan leaves are the hardest workers, converting solar energy and taking in Co2, also releasing oxygen and water vapor.

The BRANCHES
These form at nodes and will grow as the plant grows. Each branch will produce additional nodes, leaves, and a cola.

The STEM
Holds up the mighty cola bud, also the main energy and nutrition highway for the plant. It will grow straight towards light, but can be manipulated & trained, along with the branches.

The ROOTS
They love both air and water, extremely fibrous tertiary roots, rootlets & hairs, within the lop layers, closer to fresh air and where more nutrients are found. The thirsty exploring taproots will grow to locate ground water developing deeper down. Happy roots, bigger buds...

The general GROWTH CYCLE
Based on an outdoor plant of natural cycle, the plant will germinate early to late spring and grow throughout spring & summer. They start flowering in early Autumn also generally ready for harvest during the beginning of winter.
The cannabis plant nowadays comes in various strain phenotypes, outdoor 36weeks to indoor 9 weeks
Genotype + environment grown = phenotype

The SEEDS
Produced by the female cannabis plant, seeds keep the plants genotype saved to ensure future generations of its strain.

CANNABIS FLOWERS
Unlike a lot of plants the cannabis plant (along with a few other species) has two sexes, growing as either a female or male plant. Being a dioecious plant, this allows for genetic out-crossing and the plants genetic survival.

The FEMALE FLOWER
The first signs of the female flower will be a tiny pod with what looks like two white hairs coming out of it.
This pod is called a calyx, and will swell as the plant grows and flower blooms, along with many more forming in close proximity of each other and at node points. These female flowers un-pollinated are "Green Gold" or "Sensimilla Fruit" of the cannabis plant.

The CALYX
Also known as the cannabis pistillate flower, they form on the female plant and are filled with cannabinoids and include the other parts of the plant spectrum. The two hair-like objects are referred to as stigmas or a pistil. Besides making humans happy the calyxes primary function is to catch pollen and form a seed.

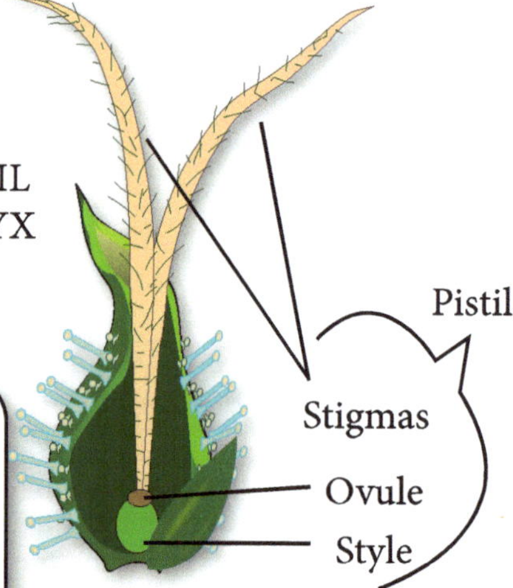

The TRICHOMES
Found largely on the flowers and sugar leaves, these lovely little cannabinoid factories help protect the flower, the terpenes smell and stickiness for bugs, fungus', weather, and as UV protection. Some types are...

The MALE FLOWER
Starts forming as a small pod or calyx containing the stamen, grouping together they look like a bunch of grapes. Once ready they start to bloom by opening up the sepals (petals) exposing the stamen anther and releasing pollen.
Once a pollen particle has engaged the female pistil, a seed will begin to form within the female calyx.

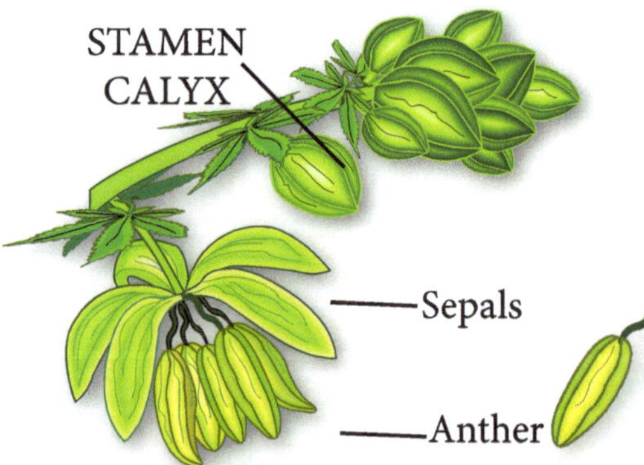

WELCOME to CANNABIS BASICS

Hello and welcome to Cannabis Basics, in this short book you will find summarized and general information with illustrations to cover the "basics" for the Southern and Northern hemispheres and controlled environments.

From seed strains to infusions, there is so much about cannabis at this point an encyclopedia could be written.

Becoming more common through the increased positive interest, growing legalizations around the world, and new findings from the in depth research and studies being done.

Cannabis is fast becoming the solution to many issues like sustainable commodities, job creation, new industry development, medical uses, some creative inspiration, and recreational fun & food tasting.

With that said hope you find this somewhat interesting and informative, and that it helps you in some way better your methods or kill some boredom.

Enjoy :)

Key info

THC -Tetrahydrocannabinol is a phytocannabinoid, recreational & medicinal.
CBD- Cannabidiol is also a phytocannabinoid, medicinal+.
MEDIUM - Growing medium is the soil or replacement mixture or water the plant grows "in".
SOLUTION - A feed mixture mainly comprising of water and soluble nutrients and solids.
INDOOR - Grown in a controlled environment & climate generally with supplemented light.
OUTDOOR - Plant grown outdoors and subject to the elements, nature, natural seasons, & light.
GREENHOUSE - Plants grown in a controlled environment while still utilizing nature & sunlight.
CANNABIS - Cannabis Sativa Species of plant.
GERMINATION -Starting or initiation of seed development.
CULTIVATION - The method of growing plants.
PROPAGATION - The breeding of specimens and cloning.
VEGGING -Vegetative the size, volume and foliage growth stage.
PRE-FLOWER - Changeover period & plant sex reveal.
FLOWERING (in bloom) - Cannabis flower fruit is growing & developing.
FULL BLOOM - Cannabis flower is peaking growth development.
RIPEN - Cannabis flower end of cycle.
NUGGET/BUD - The fruit or flower of the cannabis plant.
PHOTOSYNTHESIS - The process of capturing energy from light.
PHOTOMORPHOGENESIS - Plants response to spectrum of light.
INFUSE, PERCOLATE, STEEPING - Extraction of a material into another.
EXTRACT - Removing a material so sperate from the original material.
1 Ounce = 28.34grams,
1 Inch - 2.54cm,
1° Celsius = 33.8° Fahrenheit,
1 US Gallon = 3.785 liters
1ml = 1gram = 1000mg
10% THC per gram = 100mg/1000mg

ISBN - 978-0-620-87819-7
Issue 1
4:20 Themed Edition
Illustrated & Written by *Dylan Jowett*
Published April 2020
Copywrite & Trademarked under Info Comics
www.instagram.com/information.comics

ONCE UPON a TIME...

CANNABIS is

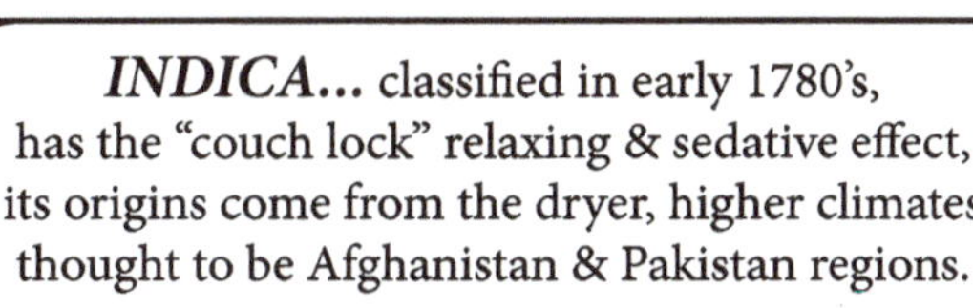

INDICA... classified in early 1780's, has the "couch lock" relaxing & sedative effect, its origins come from the dryer, higher climates thought to be Afghanistan & Pakistan regions.

Short to medium 60cm-1.5m
Closer nodes and a broad finger leaf, slightly more frost tolerant, bushier, with dense colas, flowers for 7-9 weeks.

LEGENDS - Hindu Kush, Afghani, Hawaiian Duckfoot

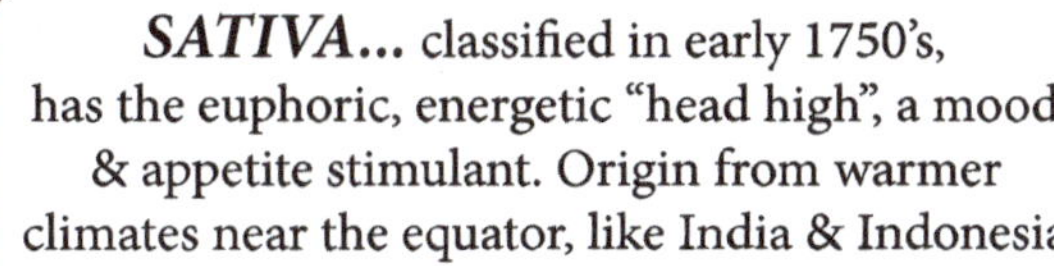

SATIVA... classified in early 1750's, has the euphoric, energetic "head high", a mood & appetite stimulant. Origin from warmer climates near the equator, like India & Indonesia

Medium to large 1.5m-3m+, dispersed nodes, longer branches, thin fingered leaves, slightly more heat tolerant, tall, big loose-packed colas, flowers 9-16 weeks.

LEGENDS - Durban Poison, Thai , Swazi Redbeard

RUDERALIS... classified in early 1920's, no real CBD or THC values. Origin from Northern Europe like Poland, Russia, and China. used in breeding for its age-driven cycle changes.

Short 30-60cm
Short finger broad leaf, more frost tolerant, not reliant on light cycle, small, no big colas. Flowers for 4-6 weeks.

HYBRID BREEDING AND AUTO-FLOWERS

HYBRIDS... experienced cultivators did it. Outdoor, Indoor, Auto-flower, the main hybrid landrace strains are bred to get the best traits to naturally come out & grow in custom setups.

Short to Large 60cm-2.5M, Customized strains, a variety available from seed banks all around the world... Australia, to South Africa, to Europe, to the Americas.

LEGENDS -Pineapple Express, WhiteWidow, BlueCheese

HEMP... Magic plant.
With cannabis, used for thousands of years, likely longer than that by ancient cultures. No THC, lots of CBD's, and endless uses.

Large to extra large 2M-5M
Similar to Sativa hemp has longer branches, thin fingered leaves, very tall, loose-packed colas, flowers 9-16 weeks.

It is the LEGEND -Turnkey commodity

GENOTYPES
The genetic traits, possibilities and properties of a strain/seed. Indica/Sativa, THC/CBD%, Regular & Feminised.

Regular:
Seeds that can grow into either male or female plants.

Feminised:
seeds that are a gauranteed 95% to be a female plant.

PHENOTYPES
Environment + Genotype = Phenotype. The conditions that bring out or enhance certain genetic traits.

Indoor
They adapted to a specific/controlled environment, a shorter growth period, and enhanced light cycle and climate.

Outdoor
Following the more natural & longer growth period and light cycle.

Auto-flower
Bred to grow very quick and not to really worry about the light cycle.

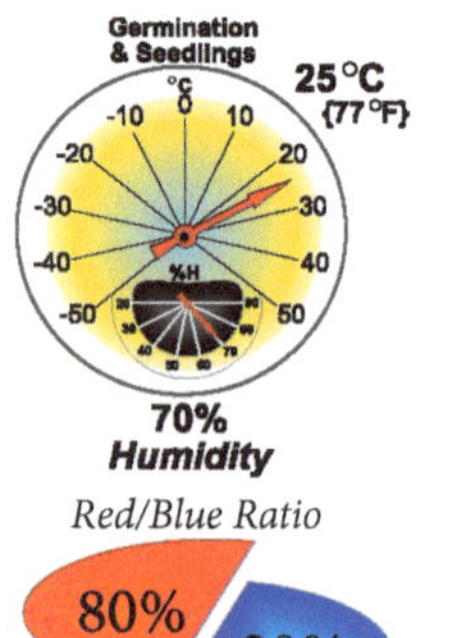

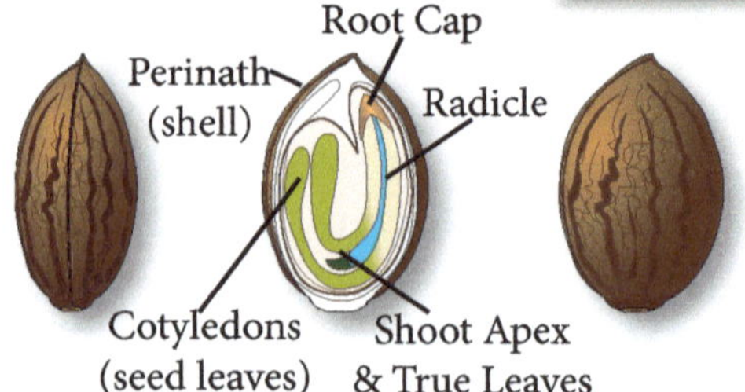

A tiny gem from where so much great cannabis comes.
The seed strains and quality vary far and wide, in short, the main 3 seed genres are...
Breed strains or Hybrids (most common),
Landrace strains of cannabis are unique and native to certain geographical areas and are mostly pure sativa's or indica's. This gives them their unique genotypes from evolving to adapt to their different climates & environments.
Heirloom strains are the rarest and the most sought after by breeders, these are generally landrace or unique bred strains that have been bred only using the best plants of the same strain.

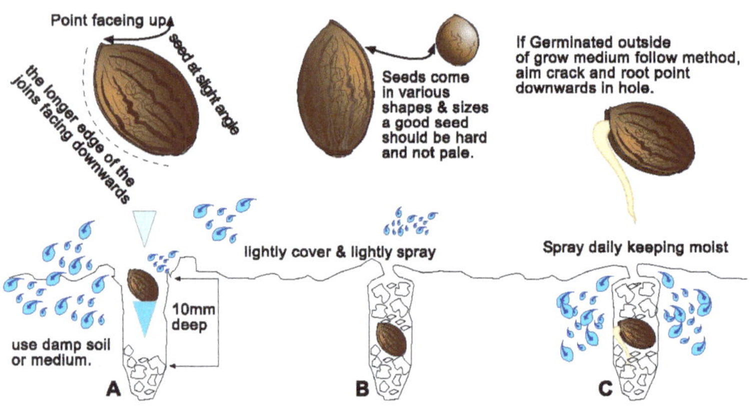

Wetting seeds is a good practice to activate them. Soak the seeds for 12-18hrs in a sideplate, add 1-2mm water, place seeds on the wet paper towel, then fold it over the seeds making a damp pocket, place another plate on top to cover. Check every 8hrs that everything is still damp and if seeds are splitting or showing root. It can take 2-5 days to show, some seeds can take 10-12 days.

Rockwool , Jiffy pellet , Soil/G.M.

Once the seed splits open and shows a little root, place the germinated seed (with the split side and root facing down), in the 5-10mm(1/5-1/3") hole made in the soil (grow medium), Rockwool, or Jiffy pellet.

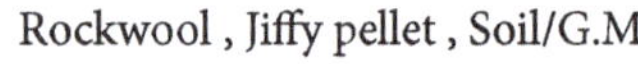

Once germination has begun the seed will split and a baby taproot will emerge. The baby taproot will curl and travel down away from the light, with gravity, looking for moisture, all while the seed will be pushed up as the sprout grows towards the light.

Once the seed sprout is happy and it has a few roots going it will pop its seed leaves out, then the first set of true (primary) leaves will start to show. Generally a ready seedling once the third node shows true leaves.

DAY 0

Cycle on a 24 week outdoor plant in soil mix

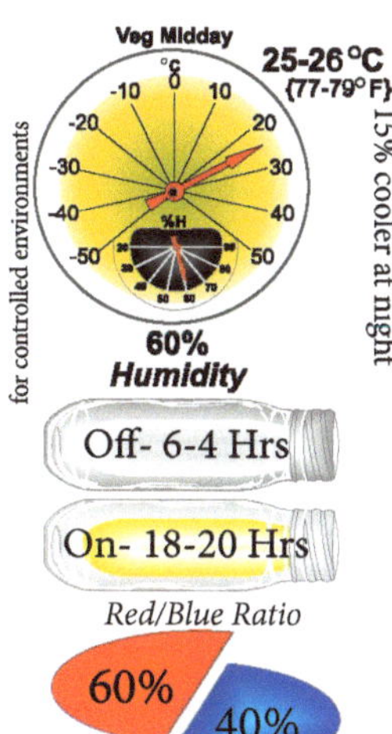

Off- 6-4 Hrs

On- 18-20 Hrs

Red/Blue Ratio

60% 40%

Water at coolest parts of the day, plants love routine even if 3 days apart. Give a cup of water 10 min before feeding solution. @temp.19.5-22.5°C @temp.67-72.5°F

Usually after Spring Equinox (North: +/-March 21, South: +/-September 21st) once the seedling has adapted to its new home it will start to veg, pushing roots it will start to grow foliage stretching towards the light. During this stage the cannabis plant likes a lot of light, water, nutrients & minerals, and will vegetate between 4 and 18 weeks depending on phenotype.

Watering & solution feeding routine will need to be followed, to maximize root growth, plant size, and node/branch production, The majority of is height and width growth happens during the vegetation stage.

Training can be started in the early part of the vegetative stage in preparation for pre-flower & flowering.

Roots will grow as much as they can, so the medium should drain easy and allow for easy growth and yet still retain water well so the root develops efficiently.

Have the root system abundant and happy for flowering stages.

NB Reminder- Keep tools, area, and hands clean*

N Nitrogen

P Phosphorus

K Potassium

From 2 weeks in

N 2
P 1
K 2 —

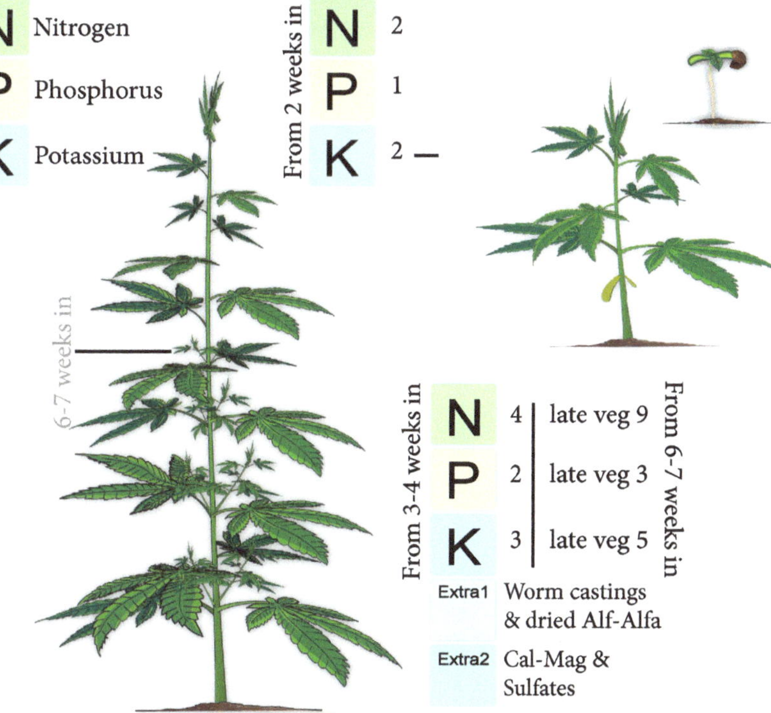

6-7 weeks in

From 3-4 weeks in | From 6-7 weeks in

N 4 | late veg 9
P 2 | late veg 3
K 3 | late veg 5

Extra1 Worm castings & dried Alf-Alfa

Extra2 Cal-Mag & Sulfates

There are a few good cannabis nutrient brands, perfect for vegging & flowering(bloom), along with ripening & flushing, choice is in research and personal preference but they do help.

The vegetation cycle naturally would begin in spring equinox (North: +/- +/- march21, South: +/- September 21) or early summer depending on the phenotype.

outdoor - sow seeds to vegetate up until just after the Summer solstice (North June 21+/- , South December 21+/-)

indoor -will simulate spring and summer light cycle (slightly extended) and climate to match.

Greenhouse hybrid- vegging in grow-box until summer solstice similar to indoor (can use daylight sun then use power lit grow area for the balance duration of light hours).

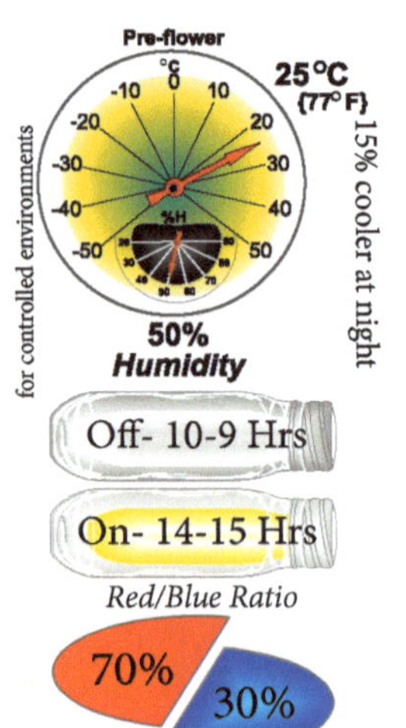

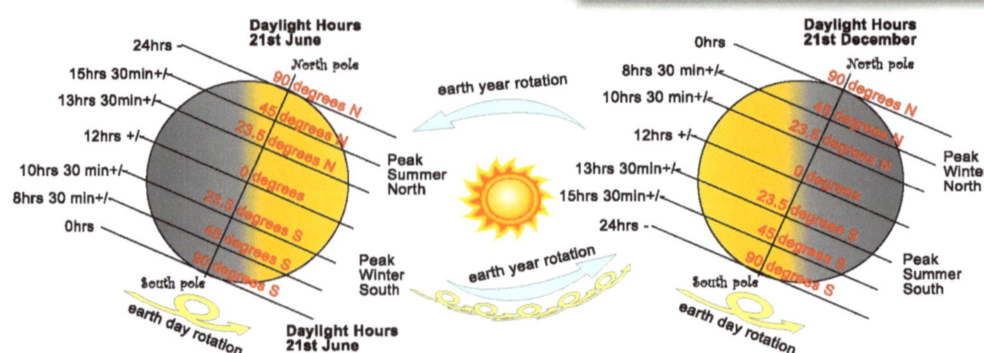

The Pre-flower begins once the daylight starts shortening after the summer solstice, some pre-flower due to age.
(North: +/- June 21st , South: +/- December 21st),
roughly 2-4 weeks after in adapting to season change.

The first signs of pre-flower will be...
flowers. Given they are not male, they will form small caylx pods with two distinct white hairs sticking out, these calyx pods start forming in clusters at the node points, beginning at the top areas of the plant.
These clusters will have more hairs (pistils) than calyx but as they develop they will swell and fatten up and cluster together more and more to start forming pre-cola buds. Pre-flower taking anything from 1 to 6 weeks. The plant will still grow & stretch its last bit during pre-flower.
Also, trichomes visible to the eye should start forming along with increased CBGA.

Pre-flower is a key point in finalizing training. During the flowering periods only small corrections should be made to trained plants.

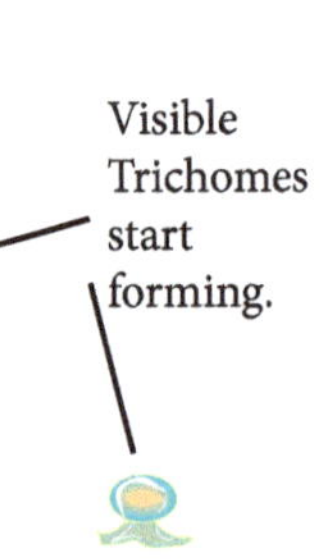

Visible Trichomes start forming.

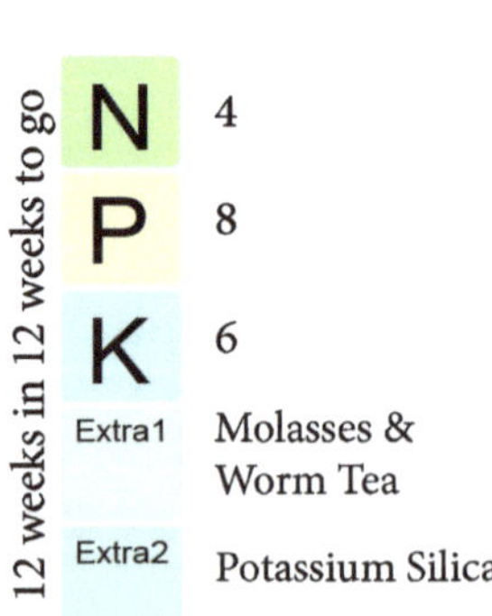

UV increase hrs for
last 5-8 weeks

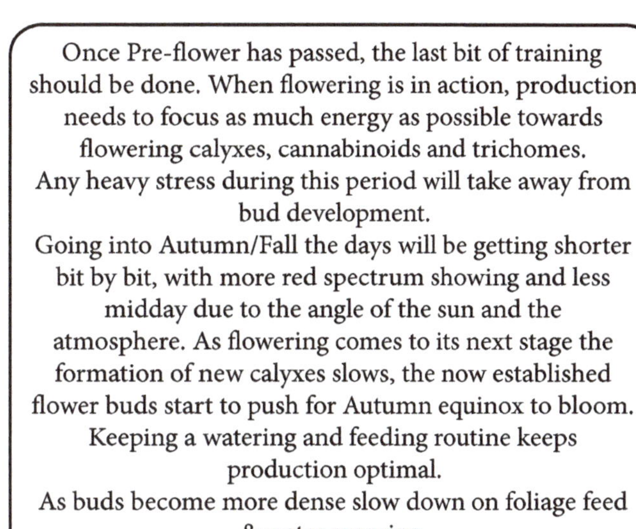

FLOWERING (Blooming)

Once Pre-flower has passed, the last bit of training should be done. When flowering is in action, production needs to focus as much energy as possible towards flowering calyxes, cannabinoids and trichomes.
Any heavy stress during this period will take away from bud development.
Going into Autumn/Fall the days will be getting shorter bit by bit, with more red spectrum showing and less midday due to the angle of the sun and the atmosphere. As flowering comes to its next stage the formation of new calyxes slows, the now established flower buds start to push for Autumn equinox to bloom.
Keeping a watering and feeding routine keeps production optimal.
As buds become more dense slow down on foliage feed & water spraying.

Possible issues...
During flowing keep eye out for pest and leaf fungus/mould.
As the plant ripens it becomes attractive to some at different stages & seasons of the year.
Mites, white aphid, & mealybugs being farmed by ants, black & white "helmets" draining the plants juices,
Caterpillars making home holes and pooping in buds & causing rot.
Buds staying damp/moist for too long will also start to rot and grow fungus or mould.
MOST IMPORTANT is NO MALE CANNABIS PLANT/FLOWERS near the flowering area. We don't want seeds taking up bud juices and weight.

Sinsemilla (no seed) bud all the way!

There are a few household items that can help with pests.
Mould : 1/3 milk +2/3 water, some mint leaves, spray and wipe, then spray again.
Pest deterrent:
1 Tbsp lemon-juice, garlic, vinegar, hydrogen perxoide, dishwashing liquid, bicarbonatde-soda + 3ltrs
(4/5 of a gallon) water then spray.
Diatomaceous earth around base in medium, dont get it in the buds.

From 10 weeks to go		
N	6	
P	15	
K	10	
Extra1	Molasses Flush every 2 weeks	
Extra2	Potassium silica & Worm castings	

BLOOM! BLOOM!

While new flowering comes to a slow and the sun is almost at its full winter angle, climate becomes cooler and dryer. The plant will focus energy on the blooming of the developed flowers and the production of CBG & the THC & CB_'s compounds developing more rapidly.

The bigger fan leaves will be showing signs of the stomata stopping production and the plant starting more on stored energy reserves, these leaves will start to yellow and die off.

Calyxes will start to become fat and juicy for the last trichomes and cannabinoids production.

The pistils will start to go darker in colour and the trichomes will be mostly milky but still look glossy or wet.

Buds are very dense minimal to no foliage feeding.

Keep an eye on the bud for mould, fungus, or bud rot.

RIPEN

Once full bloom peaks and all cells are doing the last push on conversion, we will start to see the trichomes ripen along with the hidden juices.

At this stage watching for them all to be matte-milky and some amber. The trichomes will be there fattest, terpenes will be smelling their strongest, flavonoids at their prime, and a few pistils shriveled.

Do not water for 2 days before, then harvest early morning.

Trichomes contain the largest amount of the active terpenes and cannabinoids.

Give plants a cup of water 10 min. before feeding their solution.
temp 21°C
temp 70°F

From 6 weeks to go

N	4
P	10
K	7
Extra1	Molasses, Potassium Silica & Epsom salt.
Extra2	Flush every 2 weeks, Flush 3 days before harvest.

Once trimmed
hang in drying area at
the temparature &
humidity above. Air
must not get stuffy,
and humidity not
above. 50%

HARVEST & TRIM

First get your trimming area setup with tools and
equipment ready. Most importantly a sharp pair of
scissors or trimming shears. Harvest the plant in
manageable sections, also periodically if ripening in
layers, this all saves having sections rubbing around if
there is no space to hang cued sections for trimming.
Use some heavy duty scissors or shears to harvest, not
the sharp and pointy trimming scissors or shears.
Lay down something to catch leaves and something to
hold trimmed bud sections, wax paper or a baking tray
will work.

Trimmmming off the fan leaves and
large sugar leaves straight after harvesting
is best, as the leaves are still firm, if
harvested and left, the leaves become soft
& floppy, becoming tricky to trim.
Cut off manageable sections or branches
for trimming, about 20-30cm, aim the
section downward and start to cut off all
leaves with visible stems.
Spiraling around and down the section,
starting with big leaves first to allow for
easier trimming. Repeat until happy that
most of the leaf foliage is off.
By removing these leaves it helps the plant
during the air dry to release
liquids, chlorophyll, and acids.
If in dry climates, leave sugar leaves on to
slow it drying out too quickly.

*The trichomes and resin build up on the
trimming scissors can be smoked as a
treat. Use rubbing alcohol to clean them,
it helps when trimming quite a bit.*

*The fan leaves can be
used for compost, or
cannagars. sugar leaves
and bits can be kept &
used for extracts such as
Bubble Bag hash or Dab.*

Once bud or sections are
trimmed, they can start the
drying process, hang sections &
buds in a dark airy place. If using
a drying basket cut bud nuggets
off of branches & stem sections.
Space the buds apart to allow
airflow and avoid touching.
Prepare the drying area before
harvesting.

Hang for 2 days at the slightly higher Temperature

Hang for 2-4 days

Jar up for 1 day then dry for 1 to 2 days more.

From harvesting & trimming, the cannabis must be dried in a dark airy place, a cupboard, work shed, or garage are good places. There must be no moisture or mould around, must not have stagnant air, nor have wind. No light either.
For the first 2-3 days the temperature should be around 25°C/77°F, humidity must be kept at 50%. If in a dry climate only one day at the warmer temperature.

Check bud while it drys to make sure no mould is starting. After the first couple days the temperature can come down.

After 4-7 days, depending on climate, the buds should be dry enough. Check by bending any stem around 3mm (1/8 inch) thick, if the stem makes a crack noise and breaks partially, they are ready, if it just crackles and folds like a plastic straw its not ready yet, and if snaps like a dry match stick its a bit too dry. Drying buds will shrink in size and weight around 30-60%.

Place all buds into jars, only fill them half way then tighten lids on.
Leave jars to stand for a day @25°C/77°F. After 24hrs the buds will be slightly soft, this is slow "sweating" to even out oils and draw out left over moisture. Take all buds out and hang back up for another day or two.

Manicured trim can be smoked or used for hash or dab.

Buds should be smelling good, be slightly spongy & sound slightly crunchy.
The buds can now be manicured of all the rough bits & leaves to get them looking neat & nuggety.

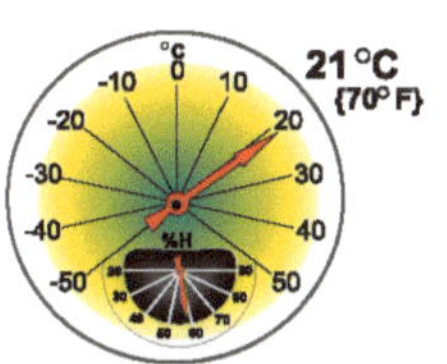

21°C
(70°F)

50- 65% Humidity

If bud is to dry or the area has a dry climate go use the higher humidity

Once bud has finished oxidizing through air drying, they can be placed in jars for "curing" (Air-Ageing).
During this process THC's and CBC produce alternate compounds. Slight decarboxulation occurs over time activating some of the compounds, terpenes become terpenoids and their smells set in. Excess chlorophyll is released along with the left over moisture building up in the jar, which will then need to be opened and the build up cycled out for fresh air.

The bud can be smoked at this point but like a fine wine's barrel-ageing, curing makes bud better with ageing and the right environment. Curing enhances and smoothens the smoking qualities and also benefits the medical and edible uses.

Burping the curing weed Jar

WEEK ONE:
Keep jar sealed for 22hrs open and leave bud out of jar for few hours then place back inside and seal jar

Keep checking for mould. For mild cases, direct sunlight out of thee jar for 10 minutes (or UV) .

Keep smelling for slight ammonia smell. Air out of jar for 2 days.

WEEK TWO:
Keep jar sealed for 23hrs, open and roll jar gently to roll bud inside, leave open for an hour then seal jar.

WEEK THREE:
Open and roll jar gently to roll bud inside, keep open for 30 minutes then seal jar.

WEEK FOUR:
Open and roll jar gently to roll bud inside open for 10 minutes (burp) then seal jar. After week four, burp jar once a week

If bud becomes too dry or crispy put a slice of orange or apple peel in the jar with the bud.

DECARBOXULATION

Decarboxulated cannabis is used mainly for recreational edibles, medicinal, homeopathic, or topical products, and other items needing the activated THC & CB_' compounds.
Preheat oven to 105°C/221°F.
Chop up cannabis until even and coarse, spread evenly over baking tray no deeper than 12mm (1/2 inch), place tray in middle of oven for 15 minutes.
Then raise temperature to 120°C/248°F for 30 minutes, then take temperature back to 140°C/275°F for 10 minutes,then remove from oven and leave to cool, or use in product straight away.
DO NOT heat above 120°C/248°F for THC or 140°C/284°F CBDs.

Heating by baking or combustion(smoking) removes the acid from the cannabinoid'ies and they become the active, decarboxulated form of the compounds.

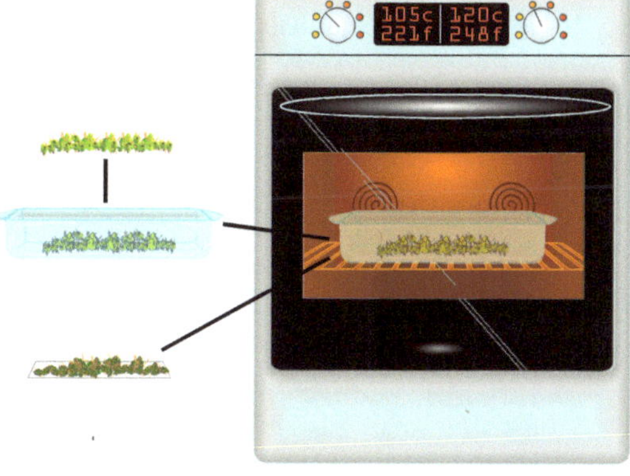

Over heating (high temprature or excessive duration) will cause thermal degradation, destroying compounds.

Extremely important, the leaf is in charge the energy for the cannabis plant to grow, they also let us know when the plant is happy or not doing well and why.
A happy plant will have firm leaves and even green colour. The happier the plant, the prouder the leaves will stand. The leaves cause the plants to grow toward and follow the right light like a magnet. The large leaves are called fan leaves, the small and smallest leaves are sugar leaves, so named for the trichomes that cover them and the high cannabinoid content. Generally if you can see the leaf stem when in full bloom it's a fan leaf, if the leaf is wedged within the bud, and can only be seen partially, thats a sugar leaf.
Sugar leaves will be covered in trichomes during flower(bloom) & ripening.

General Deficiencies

Nitrogen (N)
Used by cannabis throughout its life-cycle, a deficiency can be seen in the leaves when they start to go a pale yellow between the veins on the leaf.

Phosphorus (P)
The leaves show a blue tinge, brown spots will form, the veins and leaf stems will go a burgundy/purple.

Potassium (K)
The leaves start to go pale yellow and the ends go brown on the tips, then brown tips will start to curl.

Magnesium
The leaves start to go pale from the edges, then curl.

Sulfur
The leaves go light green and veins go pale green/yellow.

Calcium
The new leaves look pale, the stems go soft and leaves are a dark green with a mottled look.
Other common elements, Copper, Zinc, Iron, Manganese, Boron..

If climate is too hot or lights too close, the leaf ends and edges will start to go dry and curl up, even crisp and burn brown.

Lack of water or dehydration will cause leaves to wilt, sag, and hang limp and soft. Over-watered plants & leaves will droop after watering.

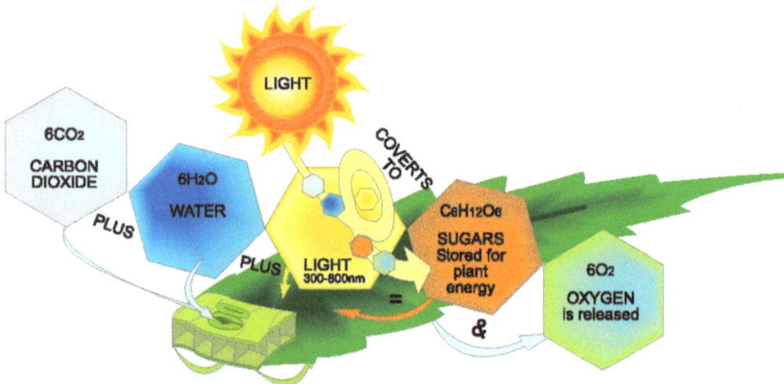

PHOTOSYNTHESIS
Photosynthesis is a process used by cannabis plant organisms to convert light energy during the daytime into chemical energy that can later be released to fuel the activity of the plant.
This chemical energy is stored in carbohydrate molecules, such as sugars, which are synthesized from carbon dioxide and water. This energy is used for the plants growth and development.

STOMATA
The cannabis leaves are covered with stomata, only found on the underside of the leaf they are not visible to the naked eye. Stomata let CO2 in and release out the converted oxygen & water vapour.
This balance continuously changes and depends on the condition of the plant, climate, and environment, all influence the regulation of the stomata.
Stomata have to be open as much as possible to let CO2 in, which is needed for photosynthesis and at the same time they have to be closed as much as possible to prevent the loss of liquids. High humidity opens up the stomata and Potassium plays an important role in opening and closing the stomata as it draws water to their cells. Plants evaporate water through open stomata to cool off, and protect themselves from dehydration by closing .
Opening (regulating) during the day and closed at night, they roughly operate for 10-12hrs.

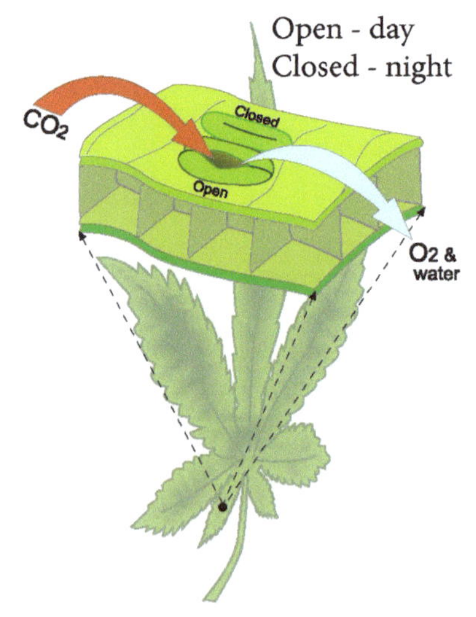

As it is with pretty much everything on the planet, water is essential to cannabis.
The watering & feeding routine should be kept as consistent as possible and done either early morning or early evening. Plants love a scheduled routine.
Water temperature should be between 19.5°C/67°F and 22.5°C/72.5°F (21°C/70°F).
PH level should be the right balance no mater which method, In soil-less and Hydroponic Systems Electrical Conductivity (EC) should be monitored frequently.
Three levels to generalize the watering technique used.
Basic - Soil & Compost - same like rain, periodically & regularly.
Intermediate - Soil-Less Medium - hybrid hydroponic system or same like rain.
Advanced - Hydroponics - a continuous cycle of water solution.

ROOTS

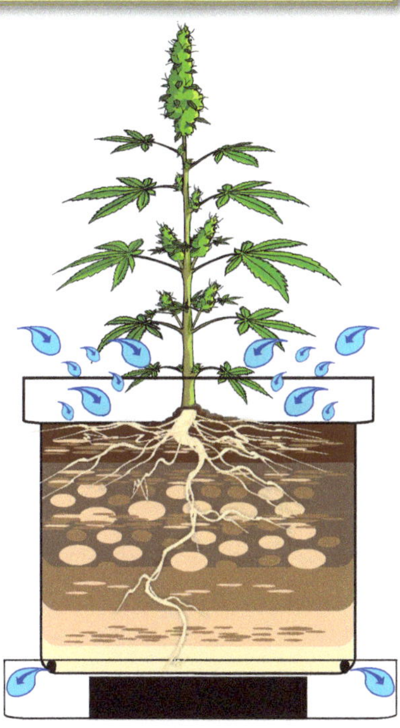

The initial part of the root which develops from the seed (radicle) will be the primary root and from that, secondary and tertiary roots develop. Most roots will be fibrous, they also form & spread within the top 25cm of grow medium.
The roots absorb food from the medium and transfer it to the rest of the plant, where it's converted into energy to carry out metabolic functions. Also, roots absorb water from the soil then deliver it to different parts of the plant.
In the beginning, they establish the plant in the soil, then provide support for the plant.
The plant doesn't stop developing roots during flowering stages, but it does it a much slower and subtle way.
This means that the root system needs to develop and be maintained as much as possible from germination.
There are two main causes usually linked to plant death: over watering and drought. Keep the watering routine consistent and even. Roots love both water and air, make sure the grown medium is loose, drains easy, and holds water well.
The roots like a temperature around 22°C/71.5°F.
Root stimulants should be stopped once flowering starts.

Soil & Compost

CoCo Husk

GROWING MEDIUMS

Perlite

Clay-Pellets

Jiffy Pellet

Rockwool

As cultivation progressed it was found that soil was not the only medium that it was possible to root plants in, of which now there are many types & combinations.
This now makes the mixes and medium layers more efficient for custom environments.
Some of the most common types for cannabis....
Soil & compost, coco husk, perlite, vermiculite, clay-pellets & water.
For clones and germinated seeds its rockwool and/or jiffy (coco/peat) pellets.
Growing mediums can be and are mixed in an array of ratios, some examples:
Soil & Compost 66%, Perlite 34% - better for "Same like Rain".
Perlite 40%, coco husk 60% - better for "Soil-Less" mostly a "drain to waste" system.
Clay pellets 70%, perlite 30% - better for "Hydroponics" more a re-circulatory system.

HYDRO - the method of growing cannabis without soil but by instead using water, minerals and nutrients, mixed to make a feed solution. Suspended and grown with only their roots exposed to the "nutrient rich" solution. Still with most the roots may be naturally supported by an inert (neutral) medium such as clay-pellets, perlite, gravel, etc...
Without soil and all its natural features, the plant is completely reliant on the hydroponic cycle and nutrients supplied, making these intricate systems to run. Soil-less growing also adopts some of the hydroponic techniques and the Drip System can be hybridized for a soil medium with no catchment cycle.
Water/Nutrient solution *level, pH* and *EC* must be monitored often and *changed regularly*.

Drip Hydroponics System
Has a growth tray suspended on top of a reservoir which is filled with water and nutrient solutions.
A water pump is placed inside the reservoir pumping water to the drip nozzles.
Dripping water keep roots hydrated but not drowning, water solution then drains back into the reservoir.
a simple system using a timer to regulate the water flow pump dripping intervals.
An air pump to keep solution oxygenated.

Nutrient Film Technique Hydroponic System
A growth tray suspended on top of a reservoir which is at a very slight angle and fed with water and nutrient solutions.
The NFT system uses a pump to deliver nutrient solution to the grow tray, continuously flowing gently supplying the roots, and draining back to recycle the unused nutrient solution.
a simple system using a timer to regulate the water flow pump, air pump to keep oxygenated.

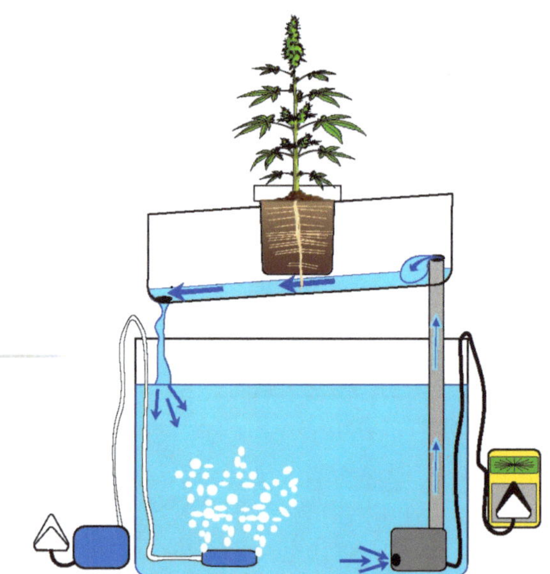

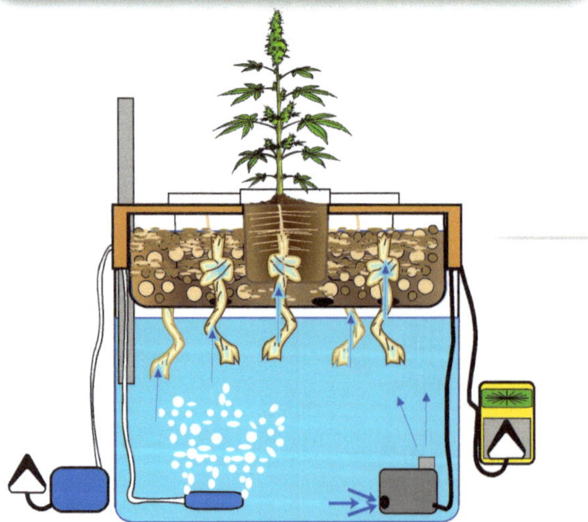

Wick Hydroponic System
Is a passive technique that does not need a water pump or mechanical movements to deliver nutrients to the plants' roots. Here nutrients move from the nutrient reservoir up the wick into the suspended grow tray and to the root system, a process known as capillary action (the same concept is used for paraffin wick candles).
A water flow pump and air pump to keep solution from going stagnant. Water level is important should be kept about 5cm(2 inchs) from grow tray.

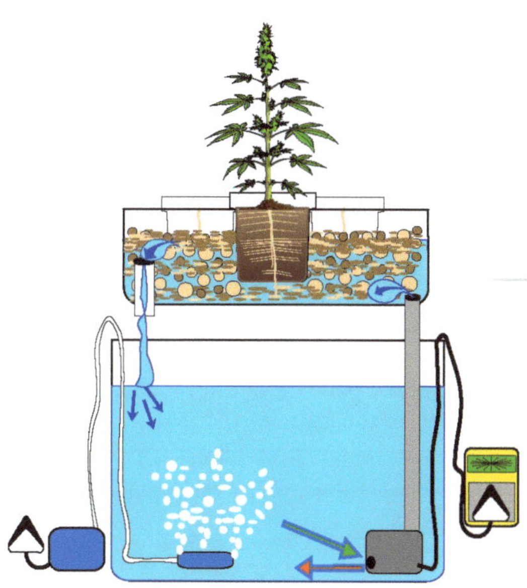

Ebb & Flow Hydroponics System
Basically means that you flood the growth reservoir and the roots of the cannabis with a nutrient solution then allow the excess to seep out back into solution reservoir. This also brings fresh air circulation to the roots since, during the flooding process, air is forced out. Longer intervals between "flooding" in comparison to Drip system.
A flood and drain is the same except it usually drains to waste not back to the reservoir.
A simple system using a timer regulates the water flow pump to stop once grow reservoir is full. When off the solution drains back down, overflow pipe for grow reservoir volume changes.
Air pump to keep solution oxygenated.

Aeroponic Hydroponic Systems
Nourishes cannabis roots with a nutrient mist. With the cannabis plant suspended above the reservoir, the roots dangle in the air as they are soaked from misting nozzles running off a high pressure water pump periodically turning off for short intervals to allow root hairs to get air.
A growing medium not essential, a basic system would use a timer to regulate the high pressure (PSI) pump, spray droplets 30-80 micron in size . roots should be damp but not dripping
A air pump keeps the solution oxygenated.

Deep Water Culture Hydroponics
Is the growing of cannabis where the roots are suspended in excessively oxygenated water and nutrients solution, growing medium not essential.
A strong air-pump and bubble defusing air-stone/s in the reservoir set below the suspended cannabis plant.
In larger capacity grow a air-stone with flow valve is set in the support pot.
CO2 can be introduced into the water via the bubble diffusers (not ultrasonic diffusers).
Water pump to keep water moving gently.
Water level needs to be monitored daily.

Natural, Organic, or Synthetic... Many different forms & types of nutrients are used to help cannabis grow to its full potential. The main "ingredient" is water but nutrients are vitally important to keeping cannabis happy... thus making you happy!
The solution mixture and feeding schedule all depend on the stage of the plants growth cycle, also the type of growing technique, environment, routine, the phenotype, and even genotype of the cannabis.
The two most important factors in the hydroponic feeding of Cannabis are:
the water solution's nutrient concentration (EC – electrical conductivity), and
the water solution's acidity level (pH). In order to have excellent cannabis growth, the nutrient concentration (EC) and pH must be consistently monitored & balanced to give the plants what they need, when they need it. A consistent solution temperature is optimal for the roots.

pH (Acidic - Alkaline)

Nutrient deficiency can stunt growth and result in a lower "BUD" yield. The correct pH allows the cannabis plant to properly access nutrients in its growing medium for better development. It is always best to do a test to determine the pH of the soil, grow medium, water and/or solution. The cannabis plant prefers a slightly acidic pH environment of about 6-6.5 pH stands for 'potential of Hydrogen' and is used for measuring the acidity or alkalinity of soluble substances within the water.
The pH scale runs from 0 to 14, Acidic to Alkaline, ideal pH will boost plant size, bud production, and even the levels of yummy cannabinoids & Terpenes.

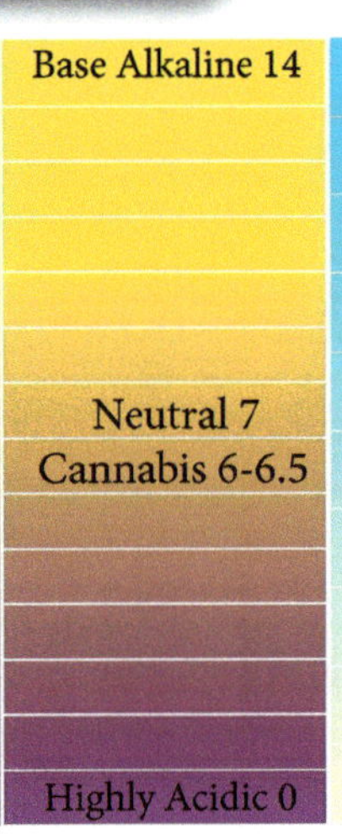

EC Low,
"Dispersed conductivity"

EC Optimal,
"Efficient conductivity"

EC High,
"Congested conductivity"

*USA 1ms/cm
(EC1.0 or CF10) =500ppm
Europe 1ms/cm
(EC1.0 or CF10) =640ppm
Australia 1ms/cm
(EC1.0 or CF10) =700ppm*

Electrical Conductivity (EC)

Used to measure the efficiency or easiness in which an electrical charge can flow through the water solution, the measuring of the EC or Electrical Conductivity can tell you if your water solution has lost nutrients or water. Also it can give you an idea of nutrient levels in the solution.
EC is measured in Siemens per Centimeter. The more salts and nutrients that are dissolved in the solution, the higher it's the electrical conductivity value. EC is used to measure PPM of TDS
EC is used mainly used with synthetic or salt based nutrients parts per million (PPM) is used for organic nutrients Total Dissolved Solids (TDS). You can add water to lower it to the original value but if EC becomes too low you should not add any nutrients to raise it, rather make a new solution as EC measurements cannot tell the difference between table salt or nutrient salts within the solution.
Check the solution once it has passed through the grow medium, as salt buildup may occur and will need to be regulated, EC can be managed for soil & aggregate grow mediums.
*NB - The EC should always be measured with a constant pH level.
Ideal EC during germination process must be between
0.4 and 0.8 millisiemens/centimeter
EC during vegetative & pre-flower stages between
0.8 and 1.8 millisiemens/centimeter
Optimal EC during flowering & blooming phase between
0.4 and 0.8 millisiemens/centimeter.
An EC measurement tool will be needed.

LUMEN

The measurement used to determine the output intensity of a light emitter: tube, lamp, bulb, even LED. The more lumen being illuminated, the more watts will be needed, the more power will be used, and more heat will be emitted from the unit. (LED's lesser so than other light types). When growing under lights a general amount of lumen is needed per square foot for a plant to grow:
Minimum range of 3000 lumen per square foot = about 40W psf.
Medium range is 5600 lumen per square foot = about 65W psf.
Optimal Range 7000+ lumen per square foot = about 90W psf.

LUX (How we "see" light scale)

The amount of luminescence (light from the light) being cast onto the surface area is measured in LUX. The light intensity on the specific surface area depends on the angle and distance from the source.
The further light has to travel the more it disperses, the lower the LUX.
(LUX = lumen divided by a square meter)

PAR & PPFD (how plants "see" light scale)

Photosynthetically Active Radiation or PAR is the photons a light source can emit in all directions. The Photosynthetic Photon Flux Density is usually referred to as PPFD.
PPFD is used to determine the number of PAR photons (range and density of the light spectrum) that land on a surface area each second, the surface area being the cannabis canopy.
PPFD & PAR more commonly used instead of lumen for measuring the LED efficiency as LED wavelength is generally narrower than that of lamps or bulbs. Plants use all spectrums of light, but some spectrums are more efficient for photosynthesis at different stages of development and for the different attributes. Basic cannabis PPFD requirements are 400 – 800 umols during the vegetative phase, and 600 – 1500 umols during flowering.
Measured in micro-moles per square meter per second (umol/m2/s).
Basically, the intensity of a colour spectrum and the amount of full colour spectrum being emited.

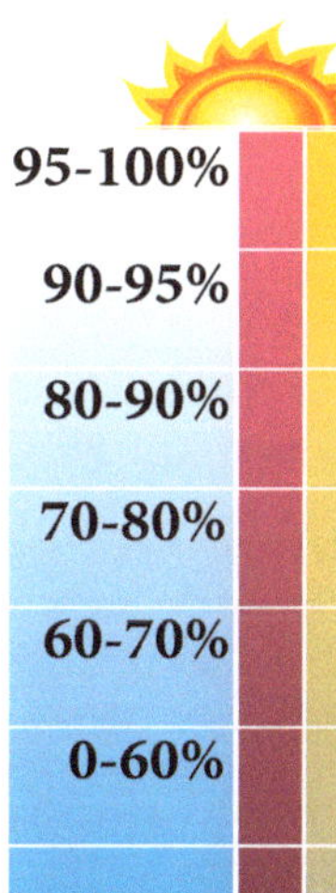

COLOR RENDERING INDEX

CRI works on a scale of 0-100% and is used to determine how accurate a light source is at rendering (showing) true colors. Under 100% CRI light you will easily notice the difference between two similar yellows, but under a 60% CRI light they will look the same color yellow. For the growing of cannabis, lamps or lights with a 90+ CRI rating should be used, especially for flowering and ripening.

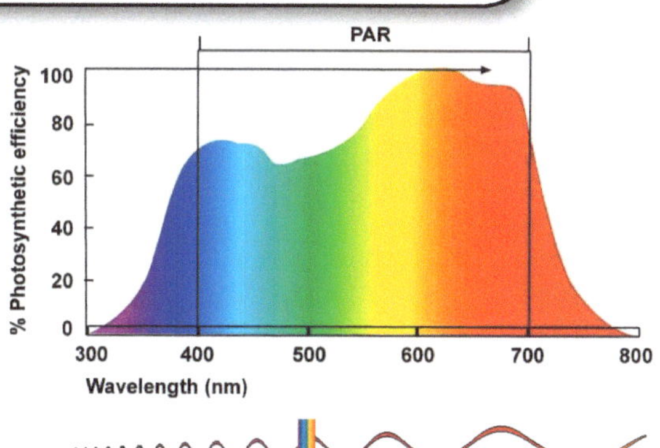

ElectroMagnetic Wavelength

Light is the visible spectrum and is a small part of the electromagnetic wavelength about 0.0035% so thats 99.9965% not seen, Everything emits some form of electromagnetic radiation. The EMW spectrum is a wide range of wavelengths from long low energy Radio wavelenghts to short high energy Gamma rays.

KELVIN (K)

The unit of measurement used to determine the color temperature of the light being emitted, like the colors from sunrise & sunset (red/orange/yellow) The midday sky (white/sky-blue/north-blue).
A basic comparison of color to heat would be like the low heat of a lighter flame to the higher heat of a blue cutting torch flame, *or* the different colors of stars such as a red dwarf or blue giant.

7000K

5600K

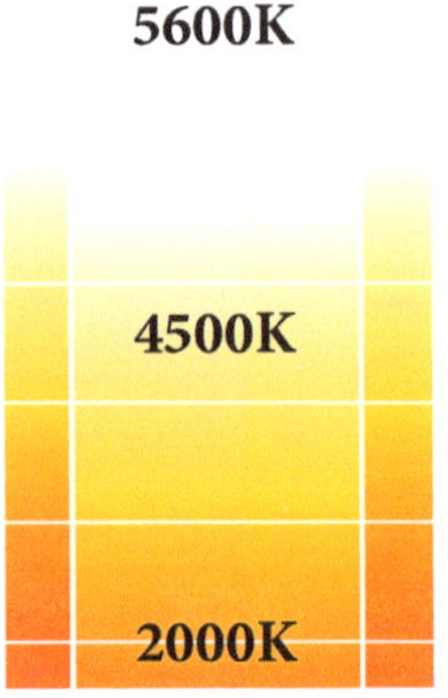

4500K

2000K

Averages

HPS lamp - 2200K
Early Sunrise & Late Sunset - 2300K
CFL/Fluorescent warmwhite - 3000K
Sunrise & Sunset - 3200K
Metal Halide lamp - 4000K
CFL/Fluorescent cool white - 4200K
Morning & Afternoon - 4500K
Daylight Metal Halide lamp - 5500k
Mercury vapor clear - 5500K
Midday Daylight - 4800k to 5600K
CFL/Fluorescent daywhite - 6500K
LED lamp - 2700K to 7000K
7200 K - Overcast Day

Mercury vapor -
50 Lm/W medium heat medium power
CFL/Fluorescent -
60 Lm/W medium heat low power
Metal Halide lamp -
87 Lm/W high heat high power
LED-
90 Lm/W low heat low power
HPS lamp -
117 Lm/W high heat high power

SUN-Total lumen +/-
6840,000,000,000,000,000,000,000,000

General PHOTOMORPHOGENESIS - controlled spectrum's

Blues for vegetative stage (foliage& roots) & pre- flower 400/430 -450/500nm.
Green & Yellow speculated stimulant & other benefits as part of full spectrum 495-590nm.
Red & Hyper-Red for germination, pre-flower, flowering & ripening 570/600 -700nm.
Far-Red & Infrared for increase flowering & ripening for the last 15%-20% of the day cycle 700-760nm.
UV-A elevates production of terpenes, THCs, & CBDs 315-400nm (off for the sunrise & sunset of day cycle).
UV-B in very small durations midday during flowering & ripening to increase trichomes 280-315nm.
(NB* - UV rays are harmful for eyes and skin, UV-C 100-220nm is used to kill bacteria).
During vegetative stage red stretches the plant more blue stimulates closer nodes and leaf production.
During flower red for Cola flower development blue helps stomata, flavonoids, and terpenes.
UV will increase trichomes production not THC strength.
Red's will increase volume and cell mass not THC strength.
Blues show the growing plant the lights source direction.

Lights
New technology has made it possible for customed & controlled spectrum's to optimize growth, hybrid grow environments are proving to be more and more efficient.
for example:
CFL's -
Clones & Seeds.
Full spect. Metal halide -
Vegetative.
Metal halide & LED -
Pre-flower.
LED -
Flower.
LED & HPS -
Bloom & Ripen.

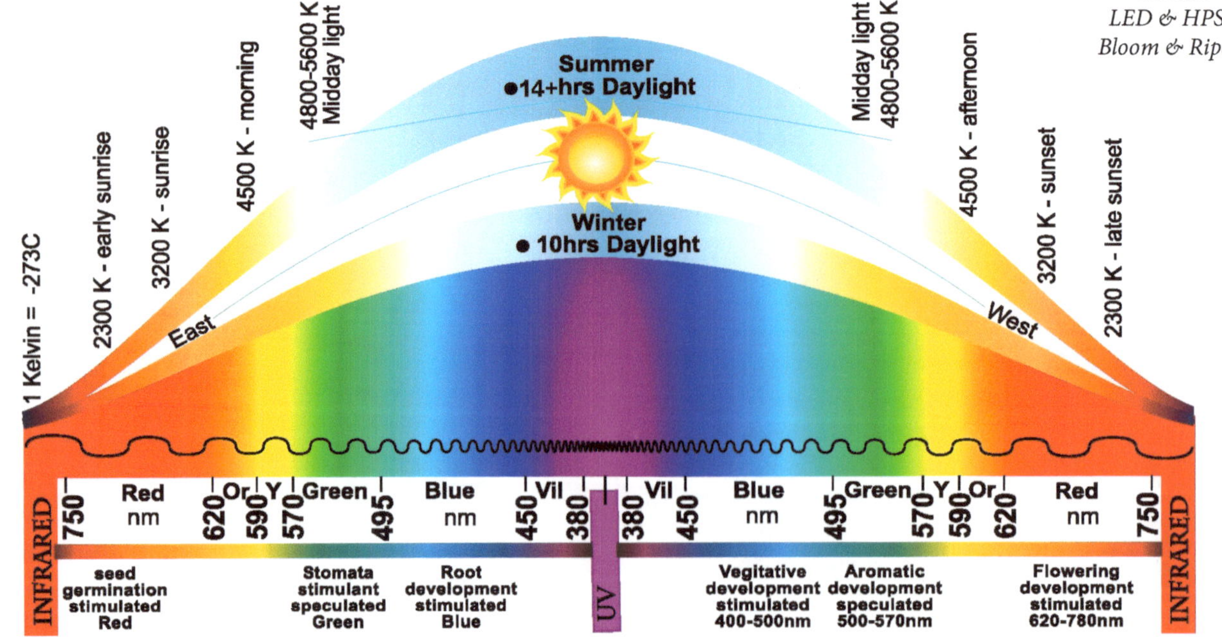

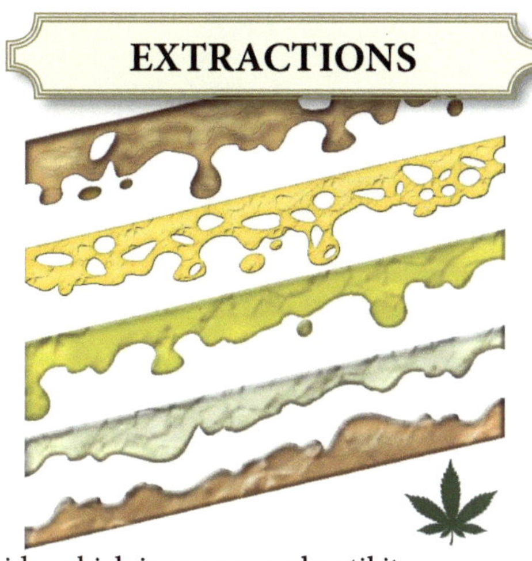

An extract is a substance gathered by extracting parts out of a raw material, often by using a solvents such as: ethanol, alcohol, butane, CO2, or water, leaving purer extract form. Extraction methods vary, some smoking methods called "DaB" or "Vaporizing" inhaling the pure form without additives. Hash(ish) back in the day, in Arabia, people used to eat it rather than smoke it.

Hash - One of the oldest, made using ice, water, or dry ice.

Kief - The collection of the tiny, sticky, white crystals known as the resin glands/trichomes.

Rosin press - Heat and pressure, together they make the resin juice run out of the bud, hash and/or kief.

Supercritical Fluid Extraction CO2 - The extracts are made using carbon dioxide, which is compressed until it creates supercritical fluid, then used to "wash" to extract the compounds.

Tinctures - Liquid concentrates made using alcohol extraction. Alcohol pulls out the cannabinoids and terpenes, the material the strained out and alcohol evaporated.

RSO Rick Simpson Oil - Soaking or steeping the cannabis plant material in pure naphtha orisopropyl alcohol, which draws out the cannabinoids.

BHO -Made using butane though different hydrocarbons (propane, butane, hexane, etc.) have been, and can be used. The final dab products can have different consistencies which is responsible for the name of the extract for example; wax, shatter, honeycomb, oil, nectar.

Molecular Separation or Distillates - Uses the extraction process "short path distillation", which separates and refines molecules and contaminants, to create a clean almost clear concentrate, with minimal thermal degradation.

Live Resin - Made from freshly harvested cannabis plants, which are frozen immediately after harvest or use straight away using some of the above methods.

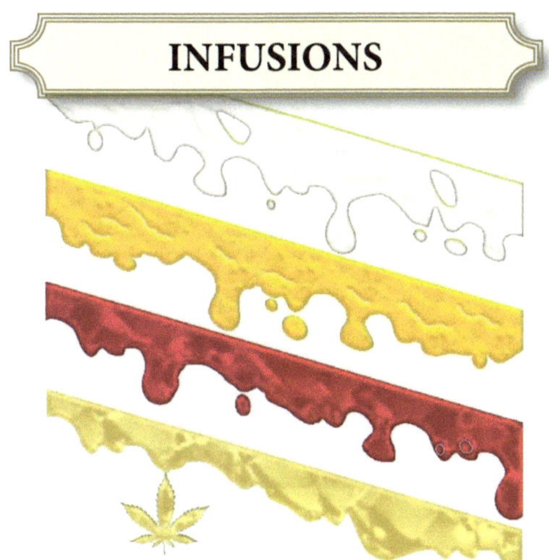

Infusions with cannabis have a few types, basic versions are: cannabis material is soaked in a substance to extract the compounds by incorporating them into the product (also known as steeping), or through the adding of an already extracted pure product to the desired product.

This is mainly done through double boiling the cannabis material or extract, done in the desired product for a required duration.

The infusions with cannabis are not always liquid in final form, generally they will be a liquid like milks, alcohols, oils, but also viscous products, such as honey, butters, creams, and jams. In some cases certain "solids" such as coffee beans, roasted nuts, and sugars.

These items are "primary" infusions, and are usually ingredients, condiments, or stronger medicinal.

Edibles would be items that includes one or more primary infusions, plus the addition of other ingredients to make up the recipe or fused product, these would be "secondary" infused products.

With infusions you get the two sides, edible recreational types and the medicinal purposed types. The same with many of the others: like salad oil or a essential oil, peanut butter or a body butter, a dessert or a beauty product...

The body creates 11-hydroxy-THC from the delta-9-THC.

When ingested passing through the liver it creates a lot more 11-hydroxy-THC than the body would with the other intake types.

ENDOCANNABINOID

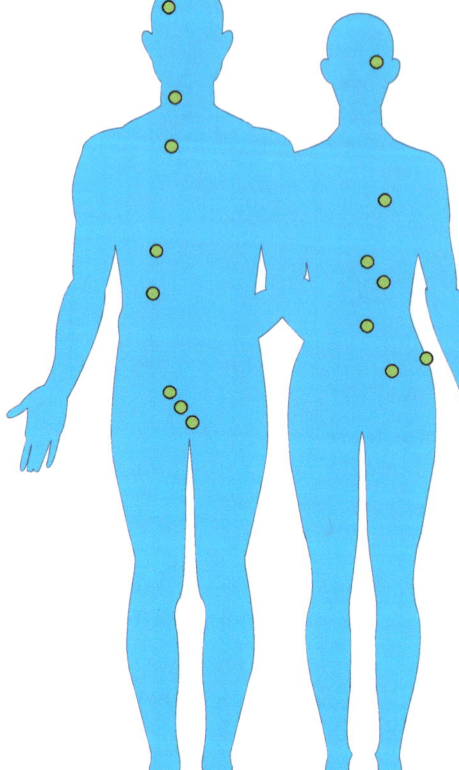

CB1 Receptors found in..
Brain/CNS/Spinal Cord
Cortical regions
Brain Stem & Cerebellum
Basal Ganglia
Olfactory Bulb
Thalamus
Hypothalamus
Pituitary
Thyroid
Upper airways
Liver
Adrenals
Ovaries
Uterus
Prostate
Testes

CB1 & CB2 Receptors found in..
Eyes
Stomach
Heart
Bones
Pancreas
Digestive Tract

Non-CB1 & Non-CB2 Cell receptors in...
Blood vessels CB1 & CB2
Lymphatic system CB2
Immune system CB2
Skin CB2

The Endocannabinoid System
Endocannabinoids are chemicals produced inside of your body, and that attach to the same receptors as some phytocannabinoids.

The ECS is a system of receptors throughout our bodies, which helps with its activities in our immune system, nervous system, some cells and the body's organs.

The receptors bridge gaps between the body & mind, they help with the body's operating efficiency, plus help to get us "High".

CBD, CBN, & THC all fit into this system like nice little keys into locks, these CBD receptors (locks) come in two types CB1 & CB2. Studies continue to find more and more compounds in cannabis that benefit humans and animals in different ways.

Inhaled into the lungs & absorbed 3-10 min,
Sublingual absorpion under tounge 10-20 min,
Oral ingestion eaten & digested 30-90 min,
Oral insertion suppository absopsion 10-60 min.

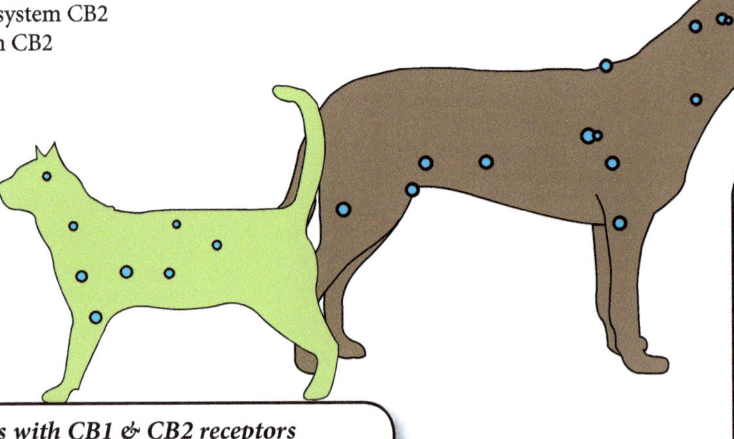

CB1 & CB2 in Dogs & Cats
CB1 -
Brain(CNS), Lungs, Vascular system, Muscles, Gastrointestinal tract, Reproductive organs.
CB1 & CB2 -
Immune system, Liver, Bone marrow, Pancreas, Brain stem.
CB2 -
Bones, Spleen, Skin, Glial cells.

Animals with CB1 & CB2 receptors
Dog , Cat , Pig , Cow , Horse , You , Rabbit , Hamster , Rat , Mouse , Kangaroo , and possibly more soon too..

The cannabis spectrum is amazing, and new discoveries will, and are being made, through the studies and analytics becoming more and more in depth.

CANNABIS PLANT SPECTRUM

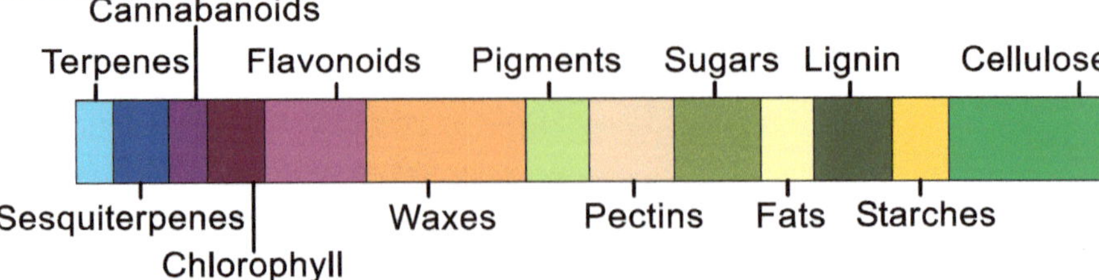

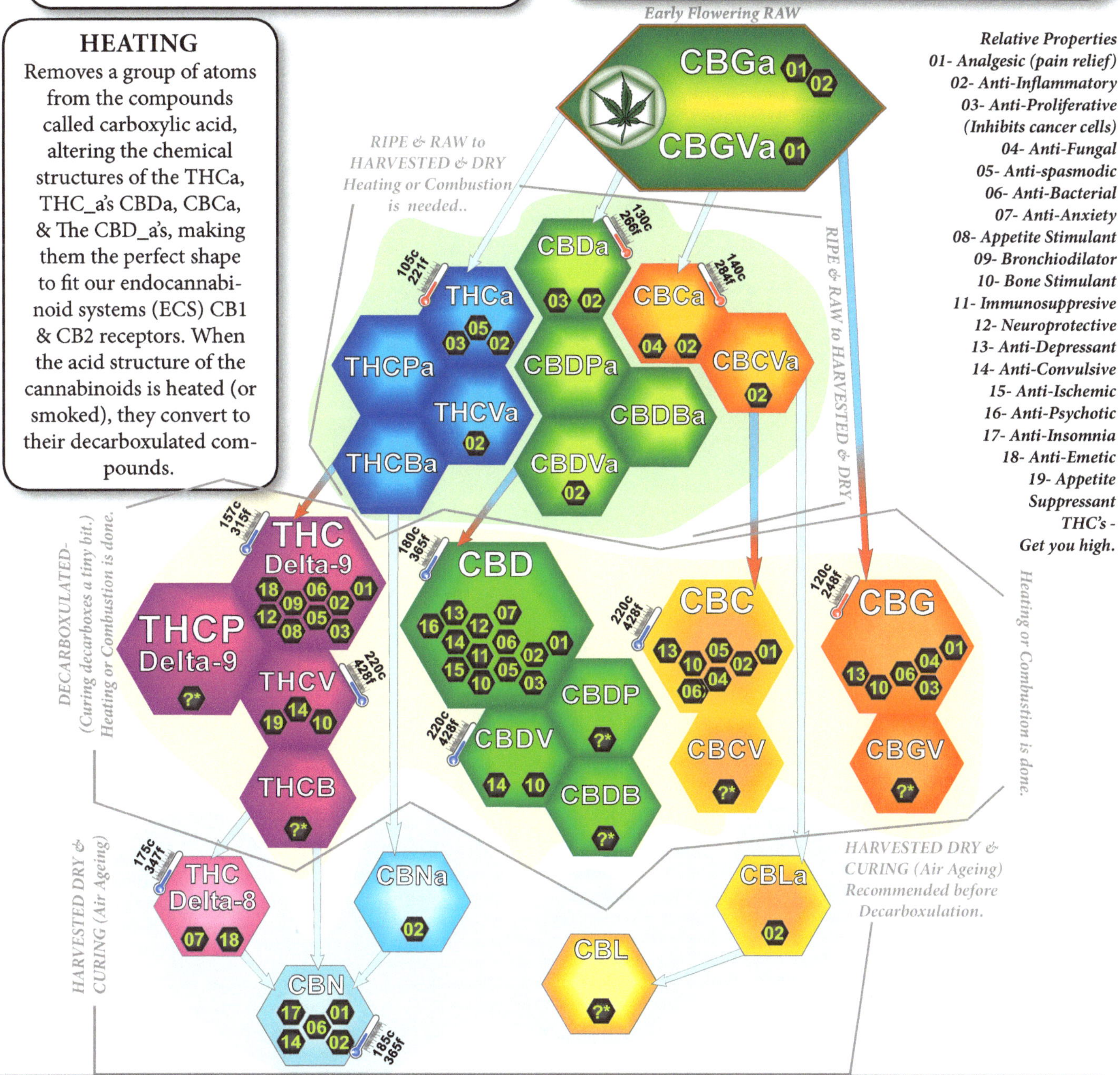

PHYTOCANNABINOIDS

There are 100+ naturally occurring cannabinoids, with more being isolated as research continues. The cannabis plant contains over 500 different natural compounds, of which the THC & CBD compounds are tie favorites, with terpenes coming in a close second, followed by flavonoids.
The entourage effect refers to the idea that the full spectrum of cannabis compounds (cannabinoids, terpenes, flavonoids, etc.) create a symbiotic enhanced effect, resulting in optimized health benefits and better "highs".

the Growth of Cannabinoids
CBGa & CBGVa are formed while cannabis grows, it happens when two organic compounds within the cannabis plant combine with each other, they are olivetolic acid and geranyl pyrophosphate. CBGa is the "foundation" building block for the rest of the cannabinoids.. THCs, CBDs, CBCs, and CBGs. The quantities of which are influence by climate conditions, cultivation, but primarily genetics.

HEATING
Removes a group of atoms from the compounds called carboxylic acid, altering the chemical structures of the THCa, THC_a's CBDa, CBCa, & The CBD_a's, making them the perfect shape to fit our endocannabinoid systems (ECS) CB1 & CB2 receptors. When the acid structure of the cannabinoids is heated (or smoked), they convert to their decarboxulated compounds.

Relative Properties
01- Analgesic (pain relief)
02- Anti-Inflammatory
03- Anti-Proliferative (Inhibits cancer cells)
04- Anti-Fungal
05- Anti-spasmodic
06- Anti-Bacterial
07- Anti-Anxiety
08- Appetite Stimulant
09- Bronchiodilator
10- Bone Stimulant
11- Immunosuppresive
12- Neuroprotective
13- Anti-Depressant
14- Anti-Convulsive
15- Anti-Ischemic
16- Anti-Psychotic
17- Anti-Insomnia
18- Anti-Emetic
19- Appetite Suppressant
THC's - Get you high.

Early Flowering RAW
CBGa 01 02
CBGVa 01

RIPE & RAW to HARVESTED & DRY Heating or Combustion is needed..
RIPE & RAW to HARVESTED & DRY

105c 221f
130c 266f
140c 284f

CBDa 03 02
THCa 05 03 02
CBCa 04 02
THCPa
CBDPa
CBCVa 02
THCVa 02
CBDBa
THCBa
CBDVa 02

DECARBOXULATED- (Curing decarboxes a tiny bit.) Heating or Combustion is done.

157c 315f
THC Delta-9
18 09 06 02 01
12 05 03
08
THCP Delta-9
THCV ?*
19 14 10
THCB ?*
220c 428f

180c 365f
CBD
16 13 12 07
14 06 01
11 05 02
15 10 05 03
CBDP ?*
CBDV 14 10
CBDB ?*
220c 428f

220c 428f
CBC
13 05 02 01
10 04
06
CBCV ?*

120c 248f
CBG
13 04 01
10 06 03
CBGV ?*

Heating or Combustion is done.

HARVESTED DRY & CURING (Air Ageing)

175c 347f
THC Delta-8
07 18

CBNa 02

HARVESTED DRY & CURING (Air Ageing) Recommended before Decarboxulation.

CBLa 02

CBL ?*

CBN
17 01
14 06 02
185c 365f

Air Ageing & Curing - The exposure to air (oxidation) and/or light (UV) causes the THCa & CBCa molecules to become CBNa & CBLa. Curing/Air Ageing converts & partially decarboxulates compounds, some better than others, in tiny amounts, and slowly. Heating will convert compounds to their decarboxulated counterparts.

Terpenes (Terpenoids)

They give us the lovely smells and tastes. The difference between terpenes and terpenoids is that terpenes are considered organic hydrocarbons, and terpenoids have additional atoms that have experienced oxidation. This happens when cannabis has been air-dried and/or cured, and can enhance or change the smell and taste profiles. Think of terpenes as "wet" & terpenoids are "dried out".

Terpenes & terpenoids are also found in fruits, vegetables, herbs, spices, even trees, and provide the essential oils of many types of medicinal plants and flowers. Also used as fragrances in some perfumes, medicine, alternative medicines such as aromatherapy & homeopathy. So far, some of the effects that have been discovered include aiding with sleep, pain relief, and having anti-inflammatory properties. There are over 200 various terpenes and terpenoids present in the cannabis plant, creating many various taste and smell cocktails.

Myrcene: Fruity citrus smell found in most varieties of cannabis. It also dictates whether a strain will have an Indica or Sativa effect. Is used in aromatherapy.

Alpha & Beta Pinene: Associated with pine trees and turpentine. Pinene (a) is the most common naturally occurring terpenoid and acts as both an anti-inflammatory and a bronchiodilator.

ß Caryophyllene: The only terpene so far that interacts with te body's CB2 ECS. It produces anti-inflammatory and analgesic effects.

Limonene: A citrus smell, found in strains with a Sativa effect. Aids in the absorption of terpenes through the skin and mucous membranes. Has been used to treat anxiety and depression.

Carene (delta-3): Sweet woody smell, helps with healing broken bones, stimulates and helps with memory.

Terpinolene: Fresh floral smell, it exhibits antioxidant and anticancer effects and a sedative effect when inhaled.

Ocimene: Has a sweet smell, it contributes to the plant's defenses and has anti-fungal properties.

Humulene: A earthy "hops" smell, acts as an appetite suppressant and shows strong anti-inflammatory abilities.

Linalool: It has a floral scent, possesses sedative properties and is an effective anxiety and stress reliever. Also been used as an analgesic and anti-epileptic.

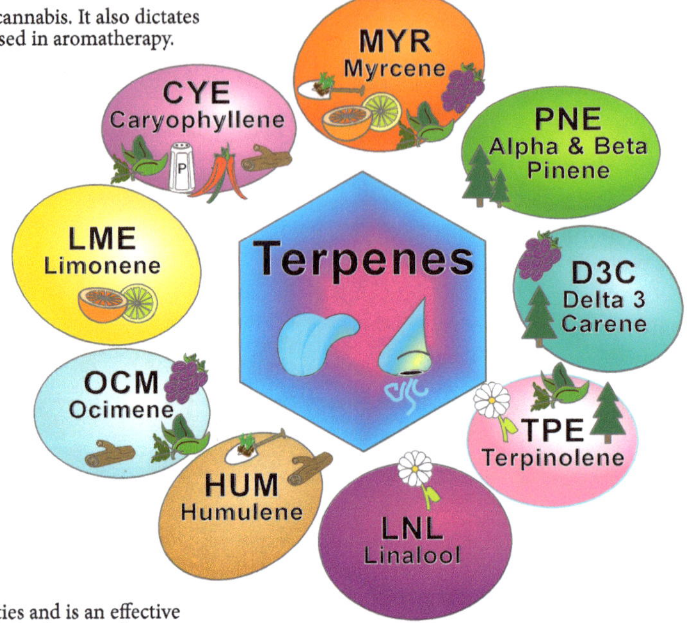

A few other Terpenes
Geraniol
Terpineol
Valencene
Phellandrene
Terpinene
Fenchol
Borneol
Bisabolol
Phytol
Camphene
Sabinene
Camphor
Isoborneol
Menthol
Cedrene
Nerolidol
Guaiol
Isopulegol
Geranyl Acetate
Cymene
Eucalyptol
Pulegone

Flavonoids

Flavonoids give us the colours in fruits, vegetables and plants, and are responsible for the colours in cannabis. They are also important to either attract pollinating insects, or repel pests, as well as act in part as UV protection. Along with flavonoids, chlorophyll, anthocyanins and carotenoids all help determine pigment outcome.

There is scientific evidence to suggest that terpenes & flavonoids work well with other cannabinoids, to boost their balancing properties in what is known as the "entourage effect". The "entourage effect" was introduced in 1998 by researchers by the names Raphael Mechoulam & Shimon Ben-Shabat. They expressed that the compounds naturally found in the cannabis plant work together better in a synergistic way to enhance, amplify and magnify their various properties. They noted that the "cannabis compounds" are not as effective when isolated by themselves.

Pigments

Colours come from genetic flavonoids and compounds besides the green from chlorophyll, but a pigment can be influenced in other ways. Acid pH favours the appearance of red colours, neutral pH favours purple colours, and alkaline pH boosts blue colours. Decreasing the number of light hours will cause a change in the colours of the leaves, a process usually called "senescence". This biological maturation leads to production of chlorophyll stopping and it focuses resources on the ripening of the flowers, causing many leaves to wither and die. Cold temperatures can also halt chlorophyll production. Anthocyanins make some plants turn purple or dark blue, if anthocyanins are low, carotenoids will appear and plants will develop the orange-yellow shades.

250M BC - Used for recreation by young dinosaurs when spying on the T-Rex.

25M BC - Inspired cavemen & woman to draw when they hot-boxed their caves.

48,000 BC - First spun into a usable fiber.

10,000 BC - Hemp shows up in pottery and cultivation in ancient Taiwan.

8,000 BC - A Hemp cloth relic is discovered in ancient Mesopotamia.

4,000 BC - Hemp is known to have been used widely in Chinese Empire.

3,500 BC - Hemp is found appearing in Egypt (they cast big molds and made pyramids :).

3,000 BC - Evidence of hemp products being used for food in China.

2,700 BC - Hemp used for medicine in China.

2,300 BC - First written record of hemp documented in a book (made of hemp).

2,000 BC - Hemp starts traveling the world at this point making friends everywhere.

1,700 BC - Egypt, Cannabis used for eye treatments.

1,600 BC - India, cannabis recorded in "Atharva Veda" for use in anxiety.

1,550 BC - Egypt, cannabis used in Obstetrics.

1,500 BC - The Shang culture show they are self sufficient agriculturally using hemp.

1,400 BC - Hemp shows up in India.

1,300 BC - Scythian's raid Europe bringing hemp with them.

1,200 BC - Plant shows up again in Egypt.

1,100 BC - The Phygrian Empire weave with hemp for their war efforts.

800 BC - The Punic people dominated the Mediterranean sea using hemp materials and products.

800 BC - Hebrews instructed to use Kaneh Bosem(cannabis) in olive oil to make Anointing Oil.

600 BC - Hemp enters Greece and Russia with human migrants and traders from Asia.

500 BC - Greek writer, Herodotus, writes extensively about hemp.

200 BC - Hemp rope (& possibly canvas) used in Greek Ships. China using stalks for arrow shafts & fibers on bows.

140 BC - Evidence suggests that China is using hemp for paper. 0-79 AD - The Roman Empire start showing them utilizing hemp.

100 AD - Samaritan gold and glass paste container containing hashish found in Siberia.

140 AD - Hemp shows up in Britain

140 AD - Chinese doctor uses cannabis as a anesthetic.

400 AD - Hemp is first cultivated in Britain

570 AD - French Queen buried in hemp

600 AD - Hempcrete used as insulation in France for timber buildings.

770 AD - First paper published book is made with hemp in China.

800 AD - The Vikings rely heavily on hemp as they invade & conquer (they introduce it to Denmark & Iceland).

900 AD - Arabic text of using cannabis juice extract to treat migraines, hash getting popular.

1000 - Hemp becomes a popular talking point in Arabia and hash is eaten frequently.

1150 - The Persian Saint Haydar finds cannabis to be inebriating and relaxing, and suggests it to all.

1253 - Garden of Cafour – Hashish hotspot in Cairo, closed by the army as public indulging too much.

1320 - Hashish smoking pipe found in Ethiopia.

1393 - Maqrizi, Egyptian historian writes of the popularity of 'Kif' (kief) among the people, social pipe smoking.

1400 - Southern Africa sees cultivation of landstrains beginning, Durban Poison, Kenya Kilimanjaro, Swazi, & Malawi

1490 - The Pope gets the paranoia and declares that cannabis is used in witchcraft.

1492 - Christopher Columbus sets hemp sails (& ropes) for new lands, gets high, gets lost, and then finds them.

1500 - Morocco begins the cultivation of their cannabis landstrain to be, Morocco Gold.

1533 - Hemp becomes compulsory to grow in Britain.

1600 - First hemp crops are cultivated in the newly found Land Columbus discovered.

1630 - Pilgrims bring some hemp to New England.

1640 - British Royal Herbalist, writes on cannabis root poultice its use on inflammation and tumors.

1700 - US farmers required to grow hemp.

1762 - Hemp is used as legal tender of trade.

1753 - Carl Linnaeus classifies Cannabis SATIVA.

1776 - The Constitution of the United States is drafted on hemp paper.

1785 - Jean-Baptiste Lamarck classifies INDICA of the Cannabis Sativa species.

1798 - Napoleon bans hemp and hashish use in Egypt.

1812 - Napoleon at war with Russia over hemp.

1842 - Irish physician, O'Shaughnessy, begins writing about marijuana for British medical journals.

1850 - Marijuana is widely used in the USA as a medicinal drug.

1850 - United States consensus finds over 8000 Hemp farms in the USA.

1890 - Most published books and papers were made from hemp up until this point.

1890 - Queen Victoria given cannabis by her physician for menstrual cramps.

1900 - Mexicans recorded using cannabis for recreational use.

1924 - D. E. Janischewsky classifies cannabis RUDERALIS.

1930 - Rastafarianism, a social movement and religion created by Jamaican preacher Leonard Howell.

1940 - Henry Ford builds the model T Ford with hemp panels and hemp bio-fuel.

1941 - Popular Mechanics features article on model T Ford and the use of Bio-fuel (hemp) that can power it.

1941 - Japans attack on Pearl Harbor cuts off US hemp supply from Philippines.

1980 - Hempcrete made in France to showcase possibilities.

1985 - Jack Herer releases book "The Emperor Wears No Clothes".

2000 - World starts taking to cannabis and hemp, legalizing begins slowly with rapid progression.

2020 - World gets high, and you read this book...

HEMP

Grown for thousands of years by so many different cultures across so many lands, hemp is a wonder of nature.

FLOWERS ——

Medicinal CDBs
Protein Powder
Extract compounds
Animal medications

Food products
Granola
Seed flour
Salad oil
Margarine
Food supplement vitamins
Cooking oils
Hops compliment(beer)
Birdseed
Protein fibers
Hemp milk

Industrial products
Fuel
Solvents
Oil paints
Varnishes
Printing inks
Lubricants
Putty
Coatings
Animal feed

Hygiene, Beauty & Cleaning
Soaps
Shampoo
Bath gels
Sunscreen base
Cosmetics
Lotions
Balms

SEEDS ——

LEAVES ——

Animal bedding (with stalk)
Mulch & Compost
Cannabacco (tobacco substitute)

STALK - FIBERS & HURDS ——

Industrial uses
Rope & twine
Nets, canvas & tarp
Carpets
Geotextiles
Fiber composites (fiberglassing)
Moulded part
Brake & clutch linings
Caulking
Cellulose (plastics)
Microfiber Cellulose
Cell fluid (abrasive chemicals)
Pyrolysis feedstock (whole)
Combustion fuel (whole)

Consumer Textiles
Diapers & tampons
Fabrics & fine fabrics
Denim
Shoes
Plastic bottles & bags
Apparel & bags

Paper-based
Printing paper
Specialty/Fine papers
Filter paper
Toilet paper
Newspaper
Cardboard
Rolling papers (smoking)

Building materials
MDF fiberboard
Insulation
Fiberglass substitute
Hempcrete cement substitute
Mortar/Stucco/Plaster

CLONE PROPAGATION

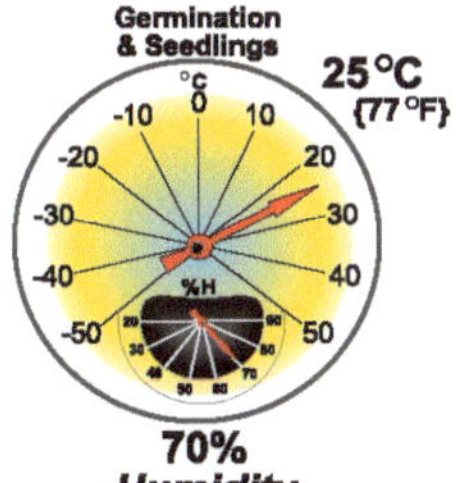

Needed:
Jar & water (300ppi pH6)
Rooting solution or powder
Humidity Dome
Rockwool or jiffy pellets
Sharp scissors
Razor or craft blade
Some perlite
Spray bottle

A clone is a cutting from a cannabis plant, which is an exact copy of a the "mother" cannabis plant. This means clones share the same genes, and will grow very similar to each other and their mother plant. Utilized mainly for "Sea of Green", a method & type of training, growing a large number of small apex cola plants, "propagated lollipopping".

Choose a spot where there is new green branching and new top node development. Being gentle not to squash the stem, cut the branch after the fourth node down and at a 45°angle.
Cuttings should be 10-20cm (5-8 inches) long. Try take clones from the lower parts of your plant and branches. Take clones during training and/or thinning the plant.

Leaving only the top leaf/leaves and cut the rest off without cutting into the stem. Place the long cutting in jar of water to rest, so the stem does not suck in an air bubble. Prepare rooting solution (if a powder, mix a little with water).

With rooting solution ready for dipping, take the long cutting, cut tips off the leaves that are left on. Using the blade, after the third node ,make a clean 45° cut, be careful not to squash the stem while cutting.
Place it in the rooting solution for 5-10 seconds.

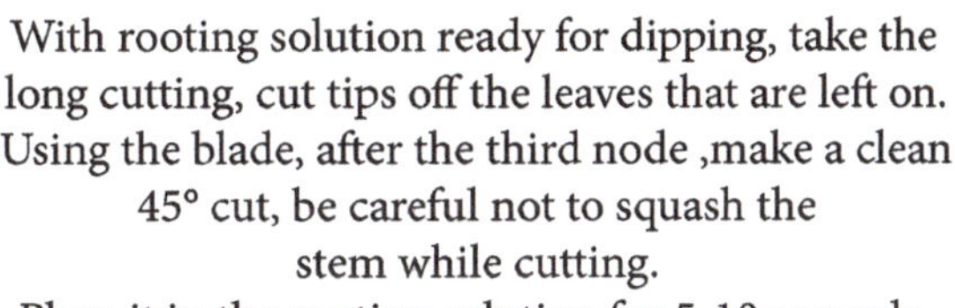

Rockwool or Jiffy pellets (pre soaked 10-15 min). Using a clean item, make the hole for the clones in the clone mediums, go about 3/4 deep.

Take clones from rooting solution and place gently in the hole just made. Using the hole-making item, gently push the medium around the clone cutting to close air gaps.
Lightly spray and place clone in humidity dome on a layer of damp perlite.
Clones like warm places so make sure you have the temperature around 25°C/77°F, & 70 - 85% humidity. Do not provide direct light to the clone for the first 12 hours.

Mother plants should be kept safe, Genetic Degeneration happens when you make a copy of a copy of a copy... The plant will get weaker and weaker with each clone generation.

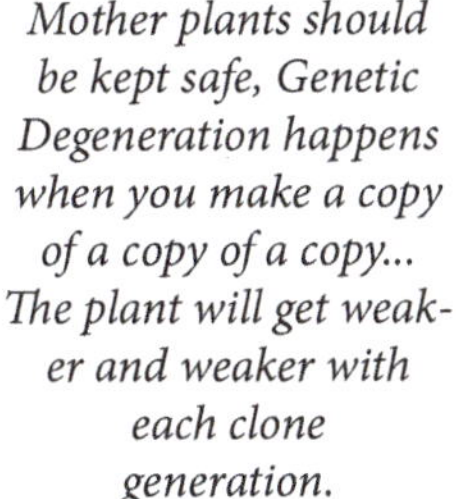

Use a more blue spectrum or cool white and make sure that the light is not too harsh/strong, or it may do damage to the clones.

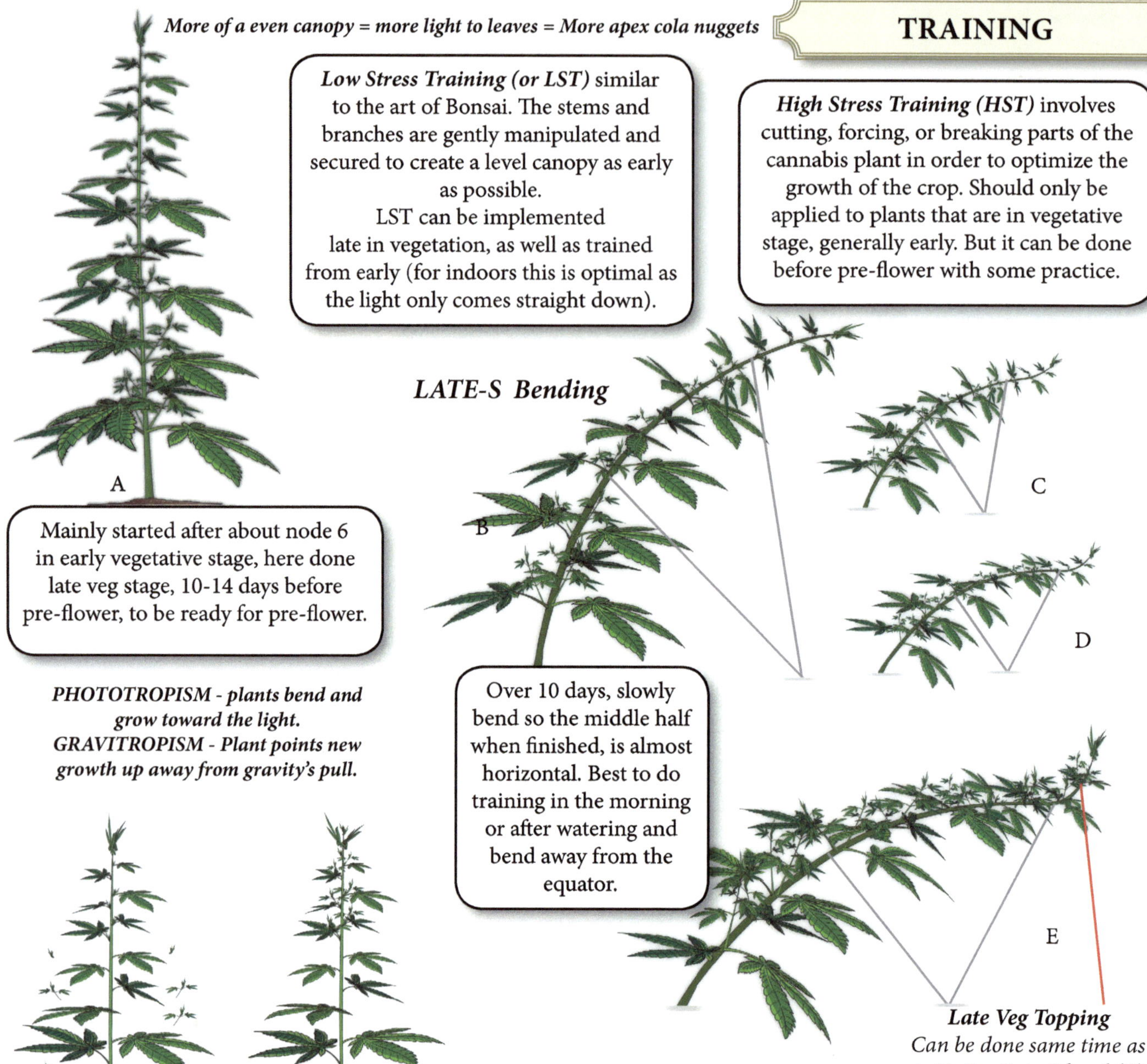

More of a even canopy = more light to leaves = More apex cola nuggets

Low Stress Training (or LST) similar to the art of Bonsai. The stems and branches are gently manipulated and secured to create a level canopy as early as possible.
LST can be implemented late in vegetation, as well as trained from early (for indoors this is optimal as the light only comes straight down).

High Stress Training (HST) involves cutting, forcing, or breaking parts of the cannabis plant in order to optimize the growth of the crop. Should only be applied to plants that are in vegetative stage, generally early. But it can be done before pre-flower with some practice.

LATE-S Bending

Mainly started after about node 6 in early vegetative stage, here done late veg stage, 10-14 days before pre-flower, to be ready for pre-flower.

PHOTOTROPISM - plants bend and grow toward the light.
GRAVITROPISM - Plant points new growth up away from gravity's pull.

Over 10 days, slowly bend so the middle half when finished, is almost horizontal. Best to do training in the morning or after watering and bend away from the equator.

Late Veg Topping
Can be done same time as initiating Late-S bend (B).

Lollipopping

Usually done mildly to get rid of lower branches taking up energy, this extreme focuses all the energy to the apex cola.
Done here late veg, most of the branches and leaves have been removed leaving the top 1/3rd. Further pruning of excess growth done just as pre-flower starts. if started to early a plant will stretch to much.

Early Topping

Done just after the 3rd node, this causes the cannabis plant to focus main growth into the branches that split at the node below the cut (top). It also causes the rest of the branches to stretch and grow a bit longer and quicker.
Combined with the other training methods, an extremely efficient training method call SCROGing is accomplished. Using a net or grid, all the tips are kept level and everything under the canopy net is cut off. New growth and stretching all are bent to stay horizontal with the net-guide for a even canaopy.

Needed:
Double boiler or two small pots
Wooden spoon
Cooking thermometer
Decaboxulated cannabis
Clothes pegs
Coffee filters
Infusion product
Glass Mason jar

1:1 – 1 cup(250ml) of oil to
1 cup of coarse cannabis
(+/-14 grams Decarb'd)

Must use *Decarboxulated* cannabis material and infused
using temperatures between 71°C/160°F- 93°C/200°F
(80°C/176°F Optimal).
Using the Double boiler method.
Add material in the beginning to percolate while coming to
temperature, Temperature must not fluctuate once reached.
14g per 250 ml cooking Oils 1-2hrs
Sun-flower, Palm, Canola
14g per 250ml tincture Oils 2-4hrs
Coconut, MCT, Glycerin
14g per 500ml Milk/s 45-60 min
(add 25 ml water per 500ml)
can use the pot lid.
28g per 500ml Honey 2-6hrs
40-45C/104-113F
(NEVER heat honey to, or above 48°C/118°F)
Simmering for 48hrs+ honey becomes caramel.
Fill a coffee filter and sew/pin the top closed so it's like a tea bag.

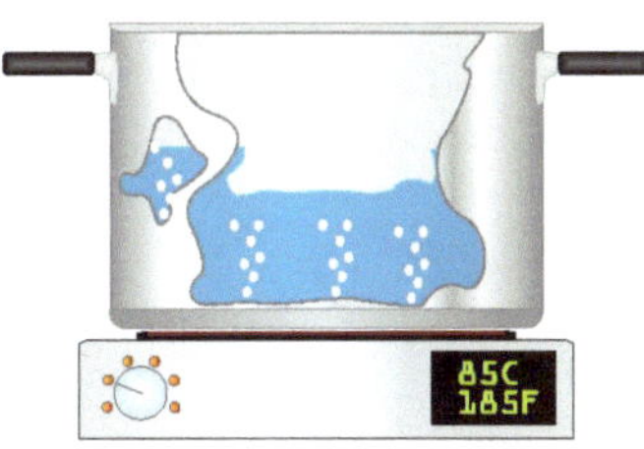

Add the Cannabis material and infusion product to the small pot, also
fill the slightly bigger pot 1/3rd full with water and place on the hot plate.
Bring the bigger pot and water to temperature then place smaller
pot into big pot, suspended in the water (not touching the bottom).
Check water level is high enough, monitor throughout the percolation period.
Monitor infusion temperature, when reached, start timing.
Monitor heat to stop fluctuations, keep stirring gently & frequently.
If water top up is needed add boiling water slowly.
Once time is up, take off heat (for honey remove and lightly squeeze
Cannabis "Tea" bag, don't squash it).
Prepare & sterilize the mason jar.
Dampen a fresh coffee filter with some infusion product then place the coffee
filer into the top of the jar, fold the edges over and use the clothes pegs to
secure it.
Start to pour the infused product through the filter into the jar.
Once done leave the cannabis material in coffee filter to gravity drain
(this filter step not done for honey).
Once drained, remove coffee filter and pegs, lightly squeeze the coffee filter,
then dispose of it with the used cannabis. Place lid on jar and refrigerate.

If needed, it is possible to double boil using
a mason jar on a dish cloth inside the water,
Caution is needed!! Try use a quality glass jar &
leave lid off, do not overheat, and
let it cool naturally.

Air pressure will cause different liquids to boil at
different temperatures.
For instance, water boils at 100°C/212°F at sea
level, about 72°C/162°F on top of Mt Everest.

Concentration Ratio
1gram =1000mg (=1ml+/-)
1gram chronic = 20%THC
20%THC = 200mg
250ml / 2.6g = 1 part per 100+/-
= 1/100.

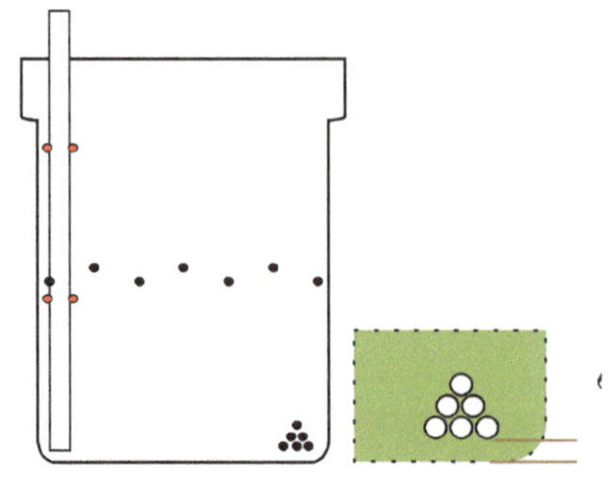

EARTH-HEMPY

This is an adaption to the "Hempy Bucket".
The aim here is to recreate the layers of the earth from topsoil down to the water table.

Compost & potting soil can be substituted with coco for the soil-less version.

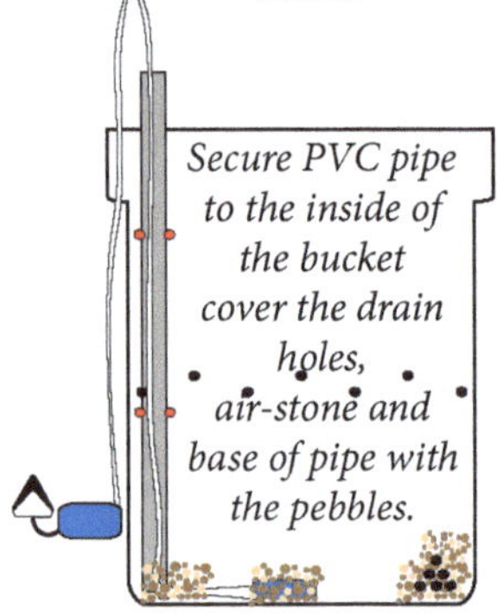

Secure PVC pipe to the inside of the bucket cover the drain holes, air-stone and base of pipe with the pebbles.

Drill 30 holes for air, evenly spaced around the bucket half way up. Then drill 4 holes (red dots) to tie the pipe in place.
On the opposite side of where the pipe will stand drill 6 draining holes
(in a triangle). the lowest part of
the bottom row of holes must be 8-10mm
(3/8 inch) up from the bottom of the bucket.

Divide the bucket into 6 Even layers from bottom to top.

6th - Mix the rest and top up before pre-flower.

5th - Poting soil & perlite 1ltr (0.3 gal) each, mixed with 2 ltr (1gallon) Compost = 4ltr.

4th - Poting soil & compost 1ltr (0.3 gal) each, mixed with 2 ltr (1gallon) perlite = 4ltr.

3rd - Poting soil & compost 0.5ltr (0.15 gal) each, mixed with 3 ltr (1gallon) perlite = 4ltr.

2nd - Poting soil 0.5ltr (0.15 gal)mixed with 3.5ltr (1gallon) perlite = 4ltr.

1st layer - clay pellets mixed with 3.5ltr (1gallon) perlite = 4ltr.

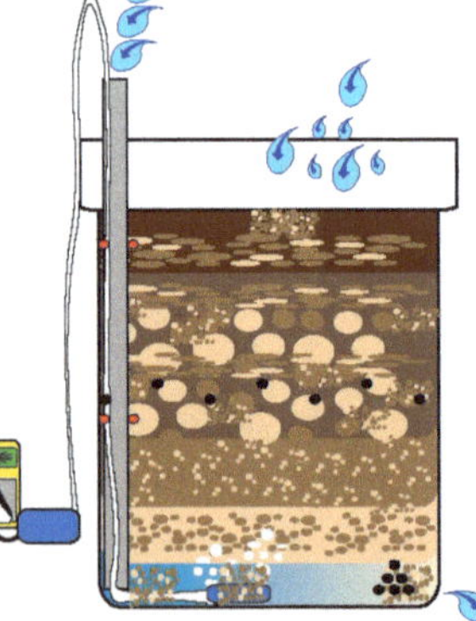

Through the PVC pipe, the water table level can be flushed efficiently, and like a "flood and drain" it will circulate air in the soil, flush minimum once a week. The air-stone pumps air into the small catchment of water below the drain holes. Run pump a minimum 4 times a day, for 15 minutes each time.
Watering the top layer with a solution, drags air down into the bucket through the top layer and air holes.
The dense top layer holds nutriens for the roots while the lower layers allow for growth, fresh water and air circulation.
Use a drip tray when feeding, and flushing.

RECREATIONAL

In all its wonderful ways THC induces a psychoactive reaction, like from joints, pipe, bong, vaporizer, dab rig, edibles and has been getting us High, Goofed, Baked, Lit, & Stoned for ages.
Some different reference names for the awesome Queen Of The Plants, Cannabis...

420, Bhangi, Blaze, Blunt, Beuh, Bowl, Bong, Boom, Bud, Cheeba, Chronic, Churus, Dabbed, Dagga, Dank, Doob, Dope, Dona Juanita, El Gallo, G, Ganja, Grass, Green, Giggly Twig, Hash/ish, Herb, HomeGrown, Hydro, J, Joint, Kief, Kush, Ma', Mary Jane, Mountain Cabbage, Marijuana, Nugget, Pot, Reefer, Sinsemilla, Skunk, Spliff, Stash, Sticky Icky OoooooWeeeeee, Stinky, Toke, Weed, Wacky Tabacky, Zol..

OUTDOOR Cannabis growers calendar - SOUTHERN Hemisphere (SA & AUS)

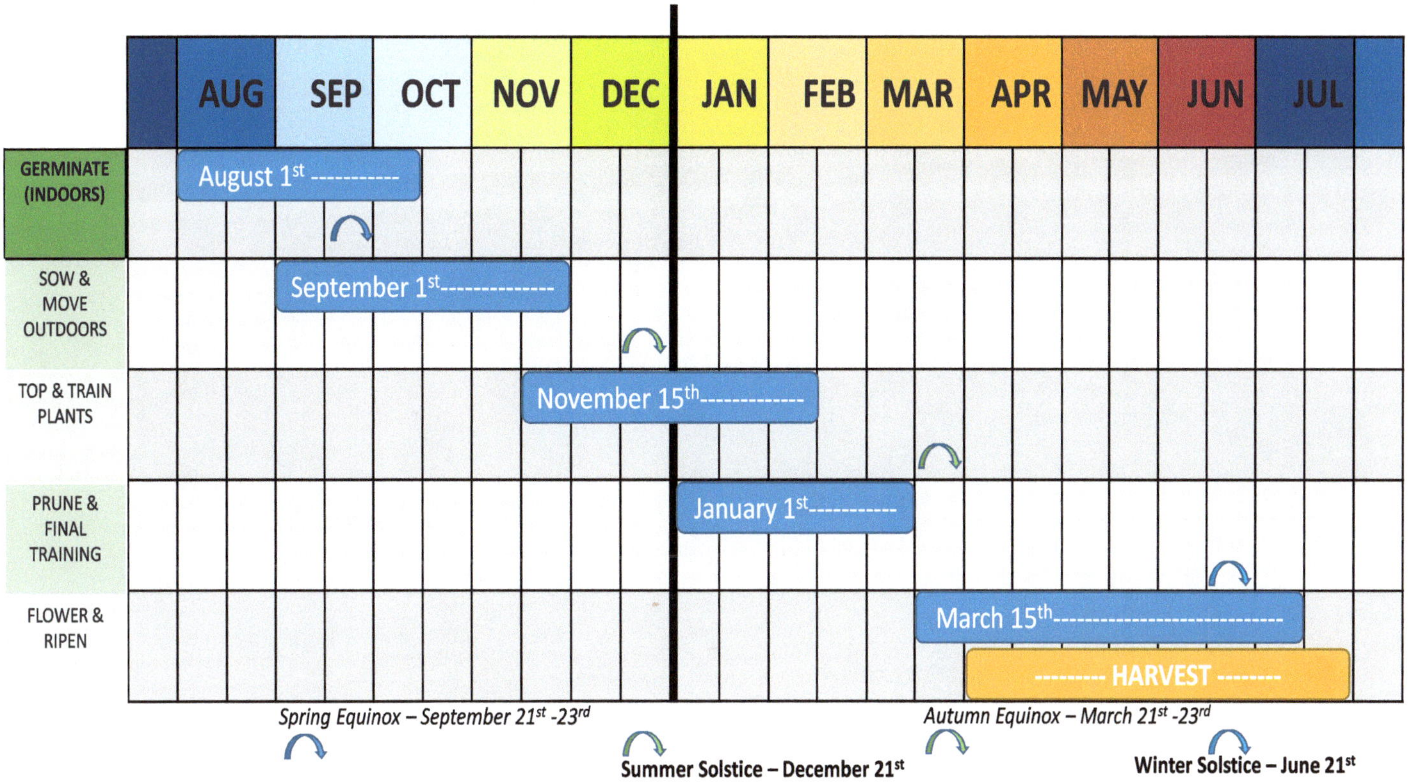

	AUG	SEP	OCT	NOV	DEC	JAN	FEB	MAR	APR	MAY	JUN	JUL
GERMINATE (INDOORS)	August 1st -----------											
SOW & MOVE OUTDOORS		September 1st-------------										
TOP & TRAIN PLANTS				November 15th-------------								
PRUNE & FINAL TRAINING						January 1st-----------						
FLOWER & RIPEN								March 15th----------------------------				
									-------- HARVEST --------			

Spring Equinox – September 21st -23rd

Autumn Equinox – March 21st -23rd

Summer Solstice – December 21st

Winter Solstice – June 21st

OUTDOOR Cannabis growers calendar - NORTHERN Hemisphere (EU & US)

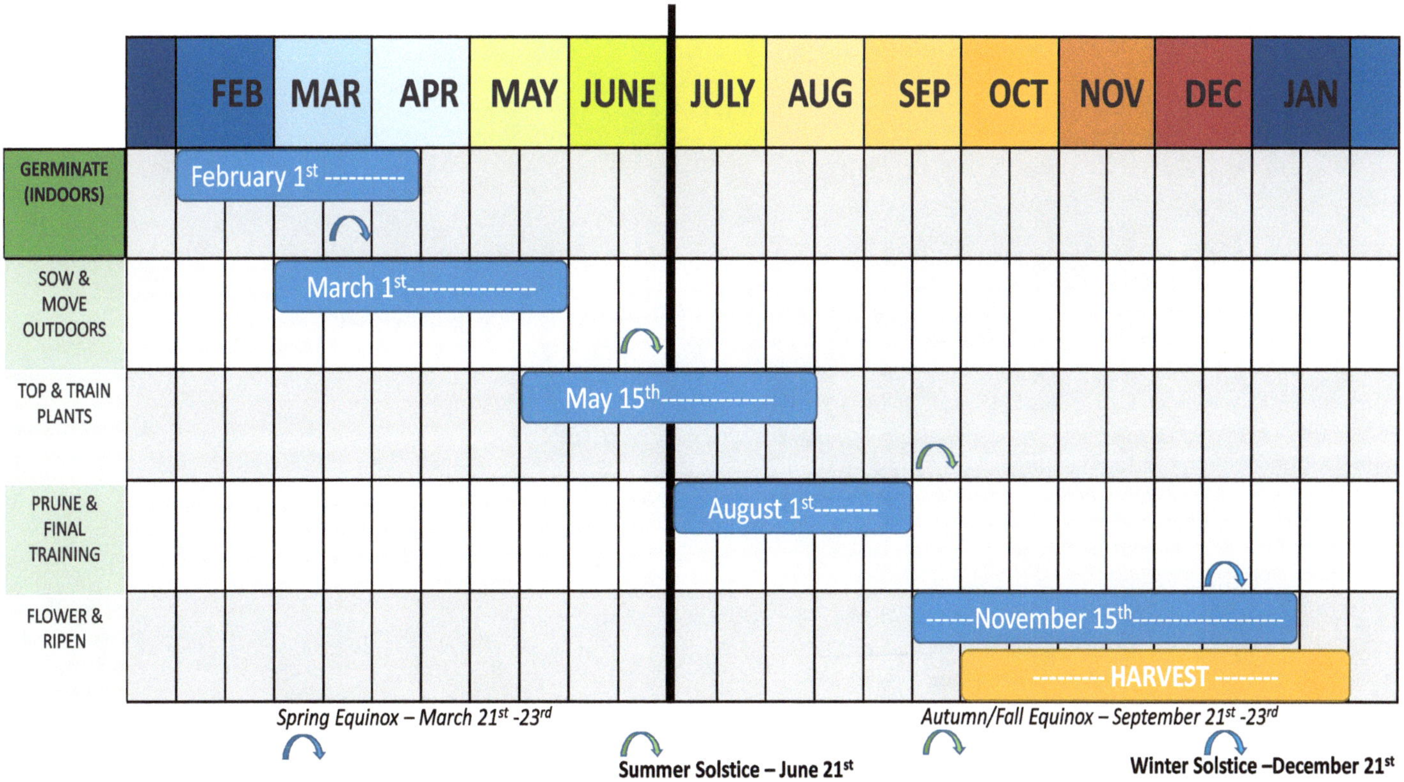

	FEB	MAR	APR	MAY	JUNE	JULY	AUG	SEP	OCT	NOV	DEC	JAN
GERMINATE (INDOORS)	February 1st ----------											
SOW & MOVE OUTDOORS		March 1st-----------------										
TOP & TRAIN PLANTS				May 15th---------------								
PRUNE & FINAL TRAINING						August 1st---------						
FLOWER & RIPEN								-----November 15th--------------------				
									--------- HARVEST --------			

Spring Equinox – March 21st -23rd

Autumn/Fall Equinox – September 21st -23rd

Summer Solstice – June 21st

Winter Solstice –December 21st

*Many thanks for reading my book, Info Comics will be back with more
printed editions & more info.
Thank You again you Lovely Humans,
grow happily ever after...
The End*

ISBN - 978-0-620-87819-7
Issue 1
4:20 Themed Edition
Illustrated & Written by *Dylan Jowett*
Published April 2020
Copywrite & Trademarked under Info Comics
www.instagram.com/information.comics

PS... I love you Mom :)

Germination: Vegitation: Training: Vegitation: Training: Pre-flower: Flower / Bloom: Ripen / Full-Bloom: Drying: Curing: Infusing : Decarboxulation:

NOTES:

Infusing : Decarboxulation: Curing: Drying: Ripen / Full-Bloom: Flower / Bloom: Pre-flower: Training: Vegitation: Training: Vegitation: Germination: